BOOKS BY JOHN TOLAND

Hitler: The Pictorial Documentary of His Life
Adolf Hitler
The Rising Sun
The Last 100 Days
The Dillinger Days
But Not in Shame
Battle: The Story of the Bulge
Ships in the Sky

HITLER
The Pictorial Documentary of His Life

JOHN TOLAND

HITLER

The Pictorial Documentary of His Life

DOUBLEDAY & COMPANY, INC., GARDEN CITY, NEW YORK
1978

Portions of this book have previously appeared in *Adolf Hitler* by John Toland.

ISBN: 0-385-04546-8
Library of Congress Catalog Card Number 77–76145

To
Carolyn Blakemore
Ken McCormick
John W. Stillman

Contents

Foreword

This book is a supplement to my biography, *Adolf Hitler,* and should help bring it to more vivid life. Since pictures can also give false impressions when taken at face value, I have written a rather lengthy commentary.

Some viewers may be appalled at the pictures depicting the horrors and destruction perpetrated by the Nazi regime. I hope everyone is appalled and I chose the most shocking examples I could locate. For these are an integral part of Hitler and National Socialist Germany. So are the photographs reflecting his achievements, the adulation of crowds, and the intimate scenes of his private life.

Hitler was a builder and a wrecker; a creator and a destroyer. He was to the end a man of the most complex contradictions. That is what I have attempted to portray.

John Toland

December 1977

HITLER
The Pictorial Documentary of His Life

ONE

"Deep Are the Roots"
1889–1918

Adolf Hitler's parents both came from the Waldviertel, a remote rural area of Austria, northwest of Vienna, not far from the present Czechoslovakian border. His father was born on June 7, 1837, in the village of Strones to an unmarried woman, Maria Anna Schicklgruber. Strones was too small to be a parish and so the baby was registered in nearby Döllersheim as Aloys Schicklgruber, "Illegitimate." The space for the father's name was blank, generating a mystery that remains unsolved, but he was probably a man from the neighborhood. However, he might have been a wealthy Jew named Frankenberger or Frankenreither, the son of the family for whom Maria Anna had worked as a domestic. In any case the Jewish family paid her support money for some years, and this later became a family scandal.

When Alois (as his name would be spelled henceforth) was five, Maria married Johann Georg Hiedler, a drifter from nearby Spital. But she died five years later and the stepfather wandered off leaving Alois to be brought up by Hiedler's brother, Johann Nepomuk Hiedler. At thirteen young Alois Schicklgruber ran away. Eventually he became a full inspector of customs, and the man who had brought him up was so proud he convinced Alois to have his name changed legally from Schicklgruber to Hiedler. On June 6, 1876, Johann Nepomuk Hiedler and three other relatives made the short trip to the town of Weitra where they falsely testified before the local notary that Hiedler's brother —they spelled his name "Hitler"—"had several times stated in their presence" that he had fathered an illegitimate son, Alois, and wanted him made his legitimate son and heir. The change of name from Hiedler to Hitler was probably to becloud the issue.

The following day Johann Nepomuk Hiedler traveled with the three relatives to Döllersheim where the original birth record of Alois was registered. The elderly parish priest affirmed from the parish marriage book that a man named Georg Hiedler had indeed married a girl named

1

Schicklgruber in 1842 and agreed to alter the birth register. With some reluctance the parish priest changed the "illegitimate" to "legitimate" and crossed out the "Schicklgruber" in the space for the child's name. In the last space he wrote in an extremely cramped hand: "It is confirmed by the undersigned that Georg Hitler whose name is here entered as Father, being well known to the undersigned, did accept paternity of the child Aloys, according to the statement of the child's mother, and did desire his name to be entered in the register of baptisms of this parish."

Alois Hitler was a strict father. His eldest son, Alois, Jr.—unable to endure his beating and discipline—ran away from home. Adolf, according to his sister Paula, also "got his sound thrashing every day" and one night tried to leave home by escaping from the upstairs window. His father caught him as he was wriggling through the narrow opening, but instead of beating chose a punishment Hitler found even harder to bear—ridicule. It took Hitler, he later confided to a friend, "a long time to get over the episode."

In 1900 Hitler started at the Realschule in Linz and did poorly. Gone for the moment was the cockiness of his village days; in the city school he seemed lost and forlorn. One day early in January 1903, his father went

1. Alois Hitler, Inspector of Customs.

into the Gasthaus Stiefler for his morning drink, remarking that he did not feel well. Moments later Alois Hitler was dead of pleural hemorrhage. The family moved to an apartment in Linz, but without his father's discipline, Adolf did even more poorly academically. He failed to graduate from high school.

In early 1908 Hitler moved to Vienna, with his friend Gustl (August) Kubizek following soon after. Gustl enrolled in the Academy of Music and was an immediate success, but Hitler failed to get into the Academy of Fine Arts and became bitter. The two youths had little money but saw many operas and haunted the museums. Hitler spent his time sketching, and writing stories and plays; he even started an opera with Gustl's help. That fall he again failed to gain admittance to the Academy of Art. Depressed, he went off on his own and when his money ran low began sleeping in bars, cheap flophouses, and the crowded "warming room" on Erdbergstrasse established by a Jewish philanthropist. By December 1909 the twenty-year-old Hitler was forced to seek charity at the Asyl für Obdachlose, a shelter for the destitute.

By the early fall of 1918 the German Army was close to defeat and there were strikes at home. Hitler was among those at the front who believed they were being betrayed by the pacifists and Jewish slackers at home who were "stabbing the Fatherland in the back." He and those like him burned to avenge such treachery: Out of all this would come the politics of the future. On October 14, 1918, Hitler was blinded by gas in Belgium and sent to a hospital in the Pomeranian town of Pasewalk.

2. Document discovered by author in Vienna in 1971 showing that Aloys was illegitimate. It also shows later alternations by the parish priest.

3. Alois Hitler himself had several illegitimate children and was twice wed before marrying Adolf Hitler's mother, Klara Pölzl, in 1885.

4. Angela, Hitler's half sister, and Alois, his half brother, with Granny.

5. The Veit family, relatives of Alois Hitler, who once advised young Josef Veit: "Drunkards, debtors, card players that lead immoral lives can't last."

6. Angela (Hitler) Raubal and son Leo.

7. The first three children of Alois and Klara Hitler died before the fourth, Adolf, was born on April 20, 1889, in Braunau on the Inn River, just across from Germany. Note his recorded name, Adolfus.

8. Baby Adolf.

9. Adolf and mother.

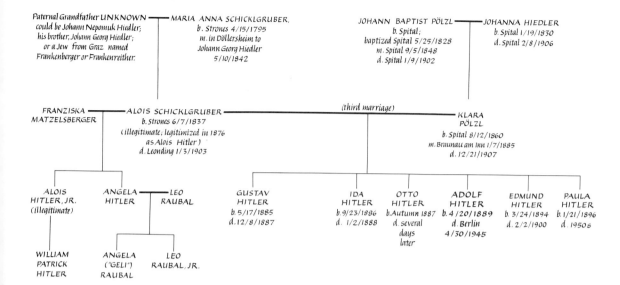

Paternal Grandfather UNKNOWN
could be Johann Nepomuk Hiedler;
his brother, Johann Georg Hiedler;
or a Jew from Graz named
Frankenberger or Frankenreither.

MARIA ANNA SCHICKLGRUBER,
b. Strones 4/15/1795
m. in Döllersheim to
Johann Georg Hiedler
5/10/1842

JOHANN BAPTIST PÖLZL
b. Spital;
baptized Spital 5/25/1828
m. Spital 9/5/1848
d. Spital 1/9/1902

JOHANNA HIEDLER
b. Spital 1/19/1830
d. Spital 2/8/1906

FRANZISKA
MATZELSBERGER

ALOIS SCHICKLGRUBER
b. Strones 6/7/1837
(illegitimate; legitimized in 1876
as Alois Hitler)
d. Leonding 1/3/1903

(third marriage)

KLARA
PÖLZL
b. Spital 8/12/1860
m. Braunau am Inn 1/7/1885
d. 12/21/1907

ALOIS
HITLER, JR.
(illegitimate)

ANGELA
HITLER — LEO
RAUBAL

GUSTAV
HITLER
b. 5/17/1885
d. 12/8/1887

IDA
HITLER
b. 9/23/1896
d. 1/2/1888

OTTO
HITLER
b. Autumn 1887
d. several
days
later

ADOLF
HITLER
b. 4/20/1889
d. Berlin
4/30/1945

EDMUND
HITLER
b. 3/24/1894
d. 2/2/1900

PAULA
HITLER
b. 1/21/1896
d. 1950s

WILLIAM
PATRICK
HITLER

ANGELA
("GELI")
RAUBAL

LEO
RAUBAL, JR.

10. Hitler's family tree.

11. Nazi version
of the family tree.

6

12. Angela and Adolf went to school here. The schoolmaster recalled that Adolf was "mentally very much alert, obedient but lively."

13. Adolf (top row, second from right) had excellent grades at the elementary school and also attended choir school at the monastery under the tutelage of Padre Bernhard Gröner. Hitler later told a friend that as a small boy it had been his "ardent wish to become a priest." On the way to choir school Hitler would pass by a stone arch in which the monastery's coat of arms had been carved—a swastika its most prominent feature.

14. Padre Gröner.

15. The Hitler family moved in 1898 and then again in 1899 to this house in Leonding, a suburb of Linz.

16. In the Leonding school Adolf was a success. He got good marks, learned to draw, and enjoyed himself reading Karl May's cowboy and Indian stories and then re-enacting them. When the Boer War broke out, Adolf became inspired with German nationalism and also played war. These games were influential in his life. Later he claimed that he got the idea for concentration camps from the British camps in South Africa and from American Indian reservations.

17. After Hitler became Chancellor the Karl May Museum was established near Dresden.

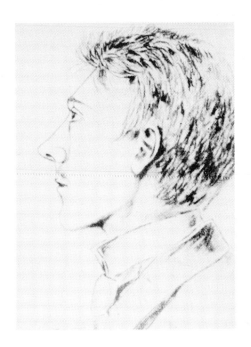

18. Hitler at sixteen as sketched by F. Sturmberger, a schoolmate who still lives in Linz. Having discontinued his studies, Adolf was enjoying the carefree life of a young Bohemian dandy. He painted, went to the opera, and daydreamed; he read voraciously, filled sketchbooks with drawings, and made plans to re-design the buildings of Linz.

19. In 1905 he finally made a real friend, Gustl Kubizek, who dreamed of being a musician. Hitler would orate for hours of his own plans to be a great architect and artist. It was like a scene from a play, recalled Kubizek. "I could only stand gaping and passive, forgetting to applaud."

20. Hitler's Certificate of Origin, 1906. Every move in Germany and Austria had to be recorded at the local police station.

21. Postwar photograph of the Spital farmhouse bedroom where Hitler and his mother slept during his happy summer vacations there. His mother was born in this house, and his father as a boy lived next door.

22. The family moved across the Danube to an apartment in the suburb of Urfahr. Early in 1907 the idyllic life of young Adolf came to an end when he learned that his beloved mother had cancer.

23. Dr. Edmund Bloch, a Jew, treated Frau Hitler. One breast was removed but the cancer persisted, so Dr. Bloch, with Hitler's permission, began a painful iodoform treatment on the open wound. Adolf nursed his mother during her last agonizing weeks; she died on December 21, 1907. This picture was taken in 1938 by order of Martin Bormann for the Führer's "personal film cassette." The inscription reads: "The Führer often sat on the chair beside the desk."

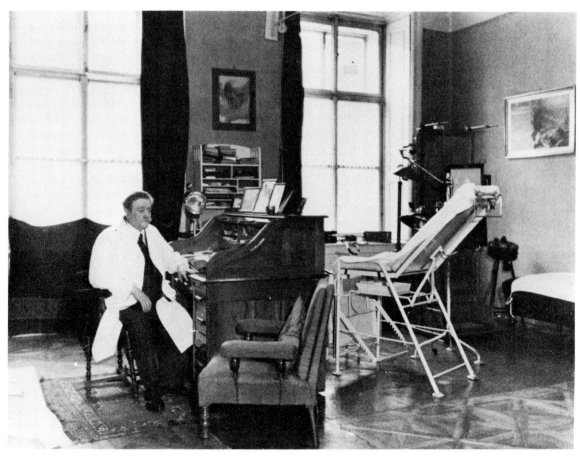

24. Asyl für Obdachlose.

25. Dormitory in the Asyl für Obdachlose.

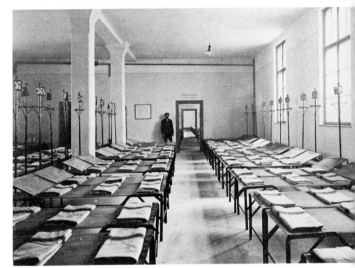

26. Hitler's sketch of Auersberg Palace, Vienna, 1911–12. Architecturally accurate, but the figures are far out of proportion.

27. On August 1, 1914, a large enthusiastic crowd at Munich's Feldherrnhalle learns that war has been declared against Russia. No one wanted war more than Hitler, the supreme German nationalist, and he enlisted in the 1st Bavarian Infantry Regiment. "I am not ashamed to say that, overcome with rapturous enthusiasm, I fell to my knees and thanked Heaven from an overflowing heart for granting me the good fortune of being allowed to live at this time." To him it meant the realization of the Greater Germany he had dreamed of since youth.

28. Military identification.

29. Hitler (seated, far right) kept his dog, Fuchsl, in the front lines for several years and taught him a variety of circus tricks such as climbing up and down a ladder. Hitler was crushed when Fuchsl was stolen in 1917. "The swine who stole my dog doesn't realize what he did to me," he wrote.

30–31. The western front, 1917–18. In December 1914 Hitler had written his landlord, Herr Popp, of his first action against the enemy: ". . . with pride I can say our regiment handled itself heroically from the first day on—we lost almost all our officers and our company has only two sergeants now."

32. Casualty announcement. On October 7, 1917, a shell exploded near Hitler, wounding him. He begged his commanding officer to let him stay with the regiment but he was evacuated to a hospital near Berlin.

33. Hitler decorated with the Iron Cross.

34. The Strasser brothers, all lieutenants. Gregor (center) later became a staunch supporter of Hitler. Otto (right) became a reluctant one, and then a sworn enemy of Nazism. The third brother, Bernhard, is now a priest in Nebraska.

35. A rare display of humor in 1918.

36. The Big Three: Field Marshal von Hindenburg, the Kaiser, and General Erich Ludendorff, the junior but dominant member of the German high command. Both Hindenburg and Ludendorff later played important roles in Hitler's career.

37. Hitler's hospital room.

38. He was treated by a psychiatrist, Professor Edmund Forster, for hysterical blindness. By early November his sight returned, but when he heard on November 9 that the Kaiser was abdicating and that the fatherland had become a republic, he again lost his sight. "That night I resolved that, if I recovered my sight, I would enter politics." As he lay in despair on his cot several nights later, he was suddenly delivered from his misery by a "supernatural vision." Like St. Joan he heard voices summoning him to save Germany. All at once "a miracle came to pass"—he could see again! And he vowed he would "become a politician and devote his energies to carrying out the command he had received."

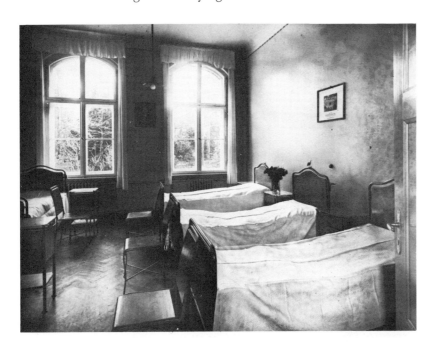

39. Defeated German troops cross the Rhine at Koblenz.

40. The Guards enter Berlin.

Birth of the Nazi Party

1918–1923

At the end of November 1918, Hitler left Pasewalk hospital and headed for Munich. He must have passed through Berlin, which was in the hands of the left-wing Spartacists. Free Corps troops, veterans of the Great War who shared with Hitler the shame of surrender and rising Communism, marched into Berlin, where most of the governmental buildings were occupied by the Spartacists, and crushed the Red centers of resistance. Berlin—eventually all of Germany—would probably have gone Communist but for the Free Corps, who also murdered the Spartacist leaders, including Rosa "Red Rose" Luxemburg.

In Munich Hitler found himself in the new Bavarian Socialist Republic. Its leader, Kurt Eisner, appeared to be the very model of a revolutionary and the tool of Moscow. He was, in fact, the very antithesis of the ruthless, pragmatic Bolshevik. He was striving for a unique kind of radical democracy. But the January 1919 elections had brought a resounding victory for the middle-class parties and a demand for Eisner's resignation.

The March Communist revolution in Hungary, led by Béla Kun, inspired one in Munich that April. In retaliation for murders of workers by attacking Free Corps troops, the Reds slaughtered some of their hostages. On May Day Free Corps troops marched into Munich to the cheers of the relieved citizenry. In vengeance these troops randomly executed more than a thousand so-called Reds.

The Red regime in Munich and the harsh Treaty of Versailles imposed on Germany a month later changed Hitler's life and turned the course of world history. He blamed Jews for the revolutions, since most of the leaders, including Rosa Luxemburg and Eisner, were Jewish. He decided to form his own political party and that autumn took over a little group calling itself the German Workers' Party. Its program was a bizarre combination of socialism, nationalism, and anti-Semitism. This moribund party, he recalled with amusement, was "nothing more than a

debating society." In quick order he transformed it into the German National Socialist Party with a rapidly growing membership.

On February 24, 1920, Hitler spoke to his first mass audience. The great Festsaal of Munich's Hofbräuhaus was jammed with almost two thousand people. Hitler presented the twenty-five-point program of the new Nazi Party. It was accepted enthusiastically and Hitler became a political force in Bavaria.

In the next two years, the Nazi Party grew into a formidable force.

Runaway inflation, the Ruhr crisis, growing resentment over the Versailles Treaty, and Mussolini's recent march on Rome inspired Hitler to stage his own march on Berlin. It began in Munich on November 9, 1923, and started from a beer hall, the Bürgerbräukeller. It ended in the death of sixteen comrades and his own imprisonment.

41. On the morning of February 21, Kurt Eisner wrote out his resignation and was en route to the Landtag to deliver it when he was assassinated by Count Anton Arco-Valley, a cavalry officer who had been refused entrance into an anti-Semitic group since his mother was Jewish.

I. Of Old Vienna. Hitler water color.

II. Ruins of Becelaere, Belgium. Hitler water color.

III. Food market and St. Peter's Church, Munich. Hitler water color.

IV. German postcards of World War I, 1914 . . .

V. . . . and 1915.

VI. "In the Beginning Was the Word," by Hoyer.

VII. During 1923, inflation was so severe that an egg could cost a million marks. Here, a five-hundred-million-mark note is converted into one for twenty billion.

VIII. Hitler Putsch, November 9, 1923, Munich. Painting by Schmitt.

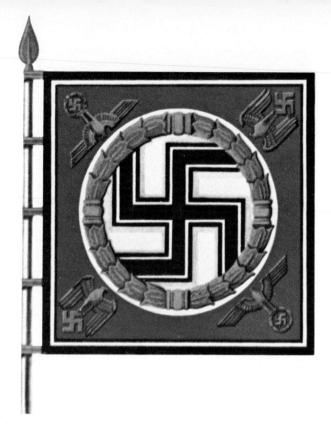

IX. "Führer Standard" for Hitler's Mercedes, designed by his private chauffeur, Colonel Kempka.

X. Detail showing the "Führer Standard" as it was mounted on the Führer auto.

XI. "High Nazi Morale amid the Rubble," by Tschech.

42–43. Revolution
in Munich, 1919.

44. Sterneckerbräu in Munich where NSDAP was founded in 1920.

45. Hitler in early party days.

46. Gottfried Feder, founder of the German Fighting League for the Breaking of Interest Slavery, inspired Hitler in the early days.

47. Dietrich Eckart—poet, playwright, drug addict, and coffeehouse intellectual —became Hitler's first mentor. He gave Hitler a trench coat, corrected his grammar, took him to good restaurants, and introduced him to influential citizens.

48. Alfred Rosenberg (wearing broad-brimmed hat) also exerted great influence on Hitler. A fanatic anti-Semite and anti-Marxist, he had brought to Munich from his native Estonia a copy of the *Protocols of the Elders of Zion*. This book purported to prove that the Jews conspired to conquer the world and was supporting evidence for Hitler's own prejudices.

49. Early party meetings at Hofbräuhaus in Munich. Gregor Strasser is at Hitler's right. To his left Franz Xavier Schwarz, party treasurer; Max Amann, the party's publisher and the Führer's former sergeant; and Ulrich Graf, the bodyguard.

50. Pistol permit issued to Hitler by the Bavarian police on November 26, 1921.

51. Leaving party meeting, circa 1922.

52. Hitler and friends at the Café Heck, one of his favorite meeting places.

53. Hitler spoke on the Marsfeld in Munich, January 28, 1923. He denounced the Treaty of Versailles: "Down with the November criminals!"

54. Hitler speaking near Munich on April 15, 1923.

55. Hitler and Julius Streicher, the virulent anti-Semite, on a Munich sidewalk.

56. Hitler and Streicher at the German Day Celebration in Nuremberg that September. The streets were a sea of Nazi and Bavarian flags as the crowd roared "Heil!" waved handkerchiefs, and tossed flowers at General Ludendorff and the marching units.

57. Preparing for the Beer Hall Putsch. Ludendorff; Dr. Friedrich Weber (wearing glasses), veterinary and leader of the Bund Oberland; and Hermann Göring, then leader of the SA.

58. The Bürgerbräukeller.

59. Göring in battle dress.

60. The Beer Hall Putsch, November 9, 1923.

THREE

A Mind in the Making

1924-1930

After the Putsch's failure, Hitler escaped to the country villa of his Harvard-educated aide, Ernst (Putzi) Hanfstaengl, where an SA doctor set his dislocated shoulder. A few days later the police arrested him there and took him to Landsberg Prison.

In Landsberg Prison Hitler, depressed and sullen, went on a hunger strike for several weeks. At first he refused even to give evidence for his coming trial.

At the trial in Munich in 1924, Hitler turned prosecutor and confounded the court. Even so he was convicted of treason and sentenced to five years in prison. On the day of the sentencing, the courtroom was crowded with women bearing flowers for their hero; several requested permission to bathe in Hitler's tub. The request was denied.

Returned to his cell at Landsberg, Hitler proselytized the warden and most of the guards. He also began dictating *Mein Kampf* to his chauffeur, Emil Maurice.

"If at the beginning of the war and during the war," Hitler declared, "twelve or fifteen thousand of these Hebraic corrupters of the nation had been subjected to poison gas . . . the sacrifice of millions at the front would not have been in vain. On the contrary, twelve thousand scoundrels eliminated at the right moment and a million orderly, worthwhile Germans might perhaps have been saved for the future."

In July 1924 when a Bohemian-German National Socialist visiting him in Landsberg Prison asked if he had changed his position concerning the Jews, Hitler replied: "Yes, yes, it is quite right that I have changed my opinion concerning the methods to fight Jewry. I have realized that up to now I have been much too soft! While working out my book I have come to the realization that in the future the most severe methods of fighting will have to be used to let us come through successfully. . . . For Juda is the plague of the world."

It took Hitler two years to rebuild the party because of dissension be-

61. Landsberg Prison.

tween its factions, and a public-speaking ban. But by 1927 he had patched the differences in the party—winning over both Gregor Strasser and Joseph Goebbels, leaders of the more Marxist-oriented northern faction—and was again permitted by the authorities to speak publicly.

Hitler's skill in speaking had improved and he now addressed himself to the basic concerns of the average German. No longer was he the racist fanatic, the frightening revolutionary, of the Beer Hall Putsch, but instead a reasonable man who sought only the welfare of the Fatherland. His "reasonable" words masked one of the most radical programs in history: conquest of Europe by any means and the elimination of the Jews. It was a program that, in one way or another, would affect the lives of most people on earth.

In September 1927, 20,000 Nazis flooded into Nuremberg for the third Party Day. There Hitler called for more living space for the German people.

62. Hitler's sister came to the prison expecting to find him despondent. "Never in my life will I forget this hour," she wrote their brother, Alois Hitler, Jr. "I spoke with him for half an hour. His spirit and soul were again at a high level. . . . That which he has accomplished is as solid as rock. The goal and the victory is only a question of time. God grant it be soon." Once more Hitler had bounced back from adversity. The discovery of this letter ended the myth that his family did not enthusiastically support his political career.

The same year he wrote another book which was not to be published in his own lifetime. Perhaps he did not want to reveal the ultimate mass-murder plan that hid behind its vague wording. Shortly after finishing this work, Hitler voluntarily visited a Munich psychiatrist, Dr. Alfred Schwenninger, to allay a "fear of cancer." This paranoid fear, along with his obsession to eliminate all Jews, persisted to the last days of Hitler's life.

63. Hitler reading in prison.

64. Hitler's cell at Landsberg.

65. Rare picture Hitler autographed while in prison.

66. With (left to right) Emil Maurice, his chauffeur; Colonel Hermann Kriebel, military commander of the Putsch; Rudolf Hess; and Dr. Friedrich Weber of the Bund Oberland. Ilse Pröhl, later Frau Hess, smuggled in the camera that took this and other prison pictures.

67. Paroled and freed in December 1924,
Hitler returned to Munich and politics.

68. One of his first visits after prison was on Christmas Eve to the Hanfstaengl's
new home, Haus Tiefland, in Herzog Park. He entertained the young son, Egon,
by imitating a World War battle, reproducing the noise of howitzers, 75s, and
machine guns. Alone with Frau Hanfstaengl, he dropped to his knees and put his
head in her lap. "If I only had someone to take care of me," he said. She asked
him why he didn't marry. "I can never marry because my life is dedicated to my
country."

69. Hitler at a meeting in party headquaters about 1925. From left to right,
Philipp Bouhler, executive secretary of the party; Arthur Ziegler; Alfred Rosen-
berg; Walter Buch; Franz Xavier Schwartz; Hitler; Gregor Strasser; Heinrich
Himmler.

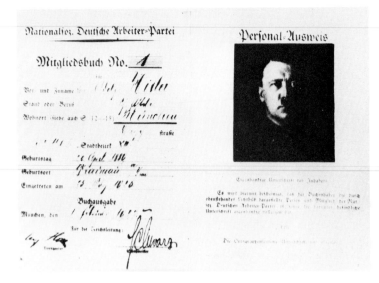

70. Hitler's first party card. He was only the seventh member, but, to make the membership look larger, it was numbered 555.

71. Hitler's party card issued in 1927 made him number one.

72. Hitler at a rally with the Blood Flag, the banner carried in the Putsch.

73. A budding Brownshirt.

74. Göring, early leader of the SA, reviewing newly formed SS troops.

75. Early picture of Hitler in full Sturmabteilung (SA) uniform. By 1930 the Brownshirt storm troopers had grown into a powerful force of 60,000.

76–78. Hitler addressing the SA.

79. Hitler fraternizing with storm troopers.

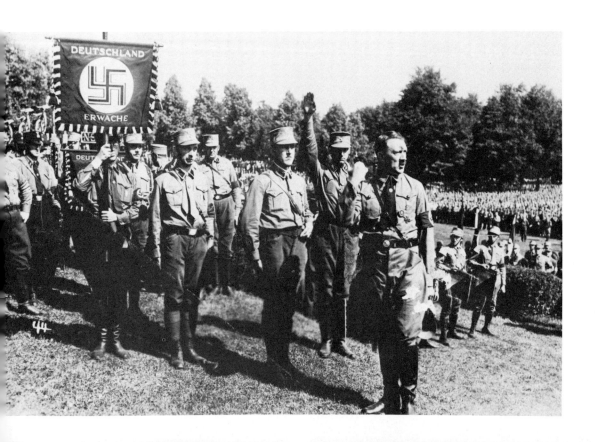

80. Horst Wessel, at left, looking over his own shoulder, the poet and future martyr of the SA.

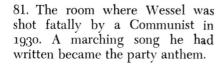

81. The room where Wessel was shot fatally by a Communist in 1930. A marching song he had written became the party anthem.

82. On January 1, 1931, the Brown House, new headquarters of the party, opened.

83. Hitler at work in his office at the Brown House.

84. Hitler liked to relax downstairs in the small refreshment room, where he sat at the "Führer" table.

85. In 1931 Hitler picked a strong leader for the SA, Ernst Röhm.

86. The rise of the Brownshirts brought on retaliation. In October 1931 the Berlin police evicted them from their barracks.

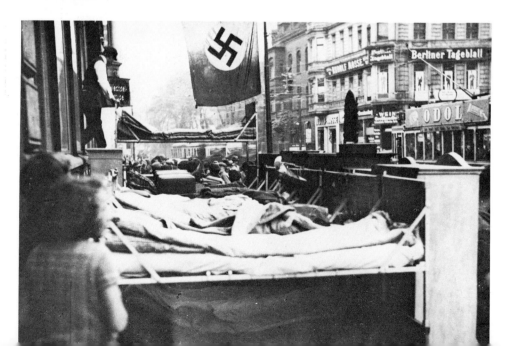

FOUR

The Loves of Adolf Hitler

The great love of Adolf Hitler's youth was Stephanie Jansten, who also lived in Urfahr. He composed numerous love poems to her, including one entitled "Hymn to the Beloved," and read them to his faithful friend, Kubizek. Adolf confessed that he had never spoken a word to her. Kubizek urged him to introduce himself, but he refused and never did more than dream about her. Fancy built on fancy. If all else failed, he told Gustl, he would kidnap her. Then in despair he decided to jump off the bridge into the Danube, taking Stephanie with him in a suicide pact. Years later it would come as a complete surprise to Stephanie to learn Germany's Führer had once been her devoted admirer.

Hitler's experience with women seems to have been limited to fantasy until he entered politics. Some early associates felt sure that Jenny Haug, sister of one of his drivers, was his mistress. She was devoted to him and reportedly carried a pistol as voluntary bodyguard. Frau Helene Hanfstaengl could not take this story seriously, and told her husband that Hitler was "a neuter." But one of his closest companions during those days disagreed. Emil Maurice, who also served as Hitler's chauffeur, claimed that they "chased girls together" and would spend time at the art academy and in artists' studios admiring models posing in the nude. Calling himself "Herr Wolf," Hitler would roam the night spots and streets for girls. As Maurice was especially attractive to women, he would act as go-between. Every so often, according to Maurice, Hitler would entertain one of these conquests-by-proxy in his little room on the Thierschstrasse. In Berchtesgaden he flirted with a sixteen-year-old girl, Mitzi Reiter. Years later Mitzi claimed that Hitler went beyond flirtation. On one walk around the lake he suddenly kissed her. "He said, 'I want to crush you.' He was full of wild passion." Before long they were lovers, and while she had visions of marriage, he only talked of renting an apartment in Munich where they could live together. During the summer of 1927, in a fit of jealousy, Mitzi tried to commit suicide by choking herself with a clothesline tied to a door.

87. Geli Raubal with her mother (left) and Paula Hitler.

88–89. Geli as a young woman.

Hitler's true love, however, was Geli Raubal, the daughter of his half sister, Angela. She was nineteen years younger and this time it was Hitler who was the jealous partner. Once he angrily objected to what she wanted to wear at the Fasching carnival. "You might as well go naked," he said, and designed a proper costume. When Hitler moved to a nine-room apartment on Prinzregentenplatz in 1929, Angela let the twenty-one-year-old Geli take a room in Uncle Alf's new lodging while pursuing her medical studies in Munich. Although maintaining the role of uncle, Hitler discreetly began to act more like a suitor. He would take her occasionally to the theater or the Café Heck. "I love Geli," he confided to a friend, "and I could marry her." At the same time he was determined to remain a bachelor. There was no doubt that Geli was impressed by her uncle's growing fame; and his fondness for her went far beyond that of an uncle. But although he deeply loved Geli it is unlikely they had sexual relations. He was too reserved to openly court any woman and too cautious to ruin his political career by taking a mistress into his own apartment—particularly the daughter of a half sister.

By 1931 Geli had become secretly engaged to Maurice, and it was

90. A postcard of Berchtesgaden sent Hitler by Geli in October 1928: "On a stroll to Berchtesgaden we came across this postcard of our house. Wolf [Hitler's dog] feels very well here, we don't have him on a leash: he always runs about free. Only his qualities as a watch dog are very poor. He has forgotten how to bark. . . . Greetings from your little niece. Geli."

known among the inner circle that they were lovers. Finally Maurice confessed to Hitler. He flew into a rage and dismissed him as his chauffeur. That summer Geli became involved with another young man, an artist from Austria, and Hitler again tried to break up the liaison. On September 17, after Hitler heard that Geli had phoned her voice teacher that she was taking no more lessons and leaving for Vienna, they had a violent argument, with Hitler storming out of the apartment to head for an important meeting in the north.

91. Early picture of Emil Maurice with Hitler in Landsberg Prison.

92. Eva Braun as a child.

93. Eva (fourth from left in bottom row) at convent school.

94. "My first Fasching costume."

95. Eva with cat.

96. Eva (left) with Hans, her first love, and her sister Gretl.

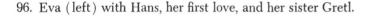

Geli locked herself in her room with instructions not to be disturbed. During the night the assistant housekeeper, Frau Reichert, heard a dull sound but thought nothing of it. But the next morning she became alarmed when she found Geli's door still locked. A locksmith opened the door. Geli was lying on the floor next to a couch, a pistol beside her. She was shot in the heart.

Hitler had just left his hotel in Nuremberg to continue his journey to Hamburg when he learned of the tragedy. He was torn with grief. For several days he went into seclusion and refused to eat. It was felt that his political life might be over. Then he came out of his depression and

97. Eva sits on a lap.

98. "Mammy!"

99. Eva meets Hitler for the first time.

100. The Führer's mistress.

101. Eva with puppies.

102. Eva's dressing table, with their photographs side by side.

headed north for the meeting. At breakfast the following morning he refused to eat a piece of ham. "It is like eating a corpse!" he told Göring. Nothing on earth, he vowed, would make him eat meat again.

Hitler's next love was Eva Braun. He had met her two years previously and occasionally took the seventeen-year-old girl to tea at the Carlton Café or a movie in Schwabing. On the day Geli had her argument with Hitler, Anny Winter, the housekeeper, had seen her angrily tear a letter in four parts. The housekeeper pieced them together and read a note from Eva to Hitler thanking him for his wonderful invitation to the theater. "I am counting the hours until I have the joy of another meeting."

In 1932 Eva, who worked at the shop of photographer Heinrich Hoffmann, became Hitler's mistress. On the first of November she shot herself with a pistol as Geli had done. While Eva had fallen desperately in love, Hitler had become so involved with the elections that he spent little time with her. To add to her misery, a rival for the Führer's affections showed her photographs of the electioneering Hitler posing with beautiful women. After writing a farewell letter to her lover, she shot herself in the neck, severing an artery. She got to the phone and gasped out to a surgeon that she had shot herself in the heart. Hitler left the campaign trail to visit the private clinic where Eva was recovering and learned from the doctor that she had done it for love of him. "Obviously I must now look after the girl," he told Hoffmann, who objected. Who could possibly blame him for what happened? "And who do you think would believe that?" said Hitler, who knew more about human nature. Also, there was no guarantee that she might not try again.

FIVE

The Brown Revolution

1932–1933

In early 1932 Hitler decided to run for President of Germany against Field Marshal Paul von Hindenburg. Still an Austrian, he hastily became a citizen of Germany through the machinations of the Nazi Minister of Interior in Braunschweig, who made him a councilor of that state.

The campaign was tumultuous, for economic depression and political rancor had turned Germany into a quasi-battlefield. Hitler appealed to both the defeated middle-aged and the idealistic youth with a simple slogan: "For Freedom and Bread." But Hindenburg remained the choice of the solid burghers and won by more than 7,000,000 votes. However, since there were many parties, the Field Marshal did not have quite a majority of the votes and a runoff election between the two leaders was necessary.

This time Hindenburg did not make a single speech, spurring rumors that he was dying, and on Sunday, April 10, Hitler got an additional 2,000,000 votes, raising his total to 13,418,051. Hindenburg raised his total by less than 700,000, yet still had a solid majority of 53 per cent. In London the *Daily Telegraph* predicted that this was the end of Adolf Hitler.

Germany was still torn by dissension, and the new government of Chancellor Franz von Papen was forced to invoke emergency powers. Using the argument that the Prussian Government could no longer deal with the Reds, Papen made himself Reich Commissioner of Prussia, which not only meant the end of parliamentary government in that state but would also set an unfortunate precedent for the future. Any political leader willing to use the emergency authority granted by the constitution could make himself dictator.

Hitler entered the Reichstag elections set for the end of July and in the last two weeks of the campaign appeared in some fifty cities, generating rabid enthusiasm wherever he went.

103. Moments earlier Hitler was made a German citizen. To his right, adjutant Schaub; to his left, adjutant Brückner and Hess.

This time the Nazis won almost 14,000,000 votes, half a million more than the combined total of their closest rivals the Social Democrats and Communists. Elated, Hitler now decided, against protests from Goebbels and Strasser, to run for Chancellor.

During the following hectic campaign, he was distracted by the attempted suicide of Eva Braun and embarrassed when Goebbels joined the Reds in a Berlin transport workers' strike. But it was not the first time that the two parties, with many goals in common, had fought together.

The election on November 6 was a disaster for Hitler. He lost more than 2,000,000 votes along with thirty-four seats in the Reichstag. The Hitler flood tide had finally ebbed and the strategy of gaining power through the ballot box had reached a dead end. Hitler is said to have threatened suicide. A month later Gregor Strasser, disgusted with Hitler's chief advisers, resigned from the Nazi Party. "Göring is a brutal egotist who cares nothing for Germany, as long as he becomes something," Strasser complained to Hans Frank. "Goebbels is a limping devil and basically two-faced, Röhm is a pig. This is the Old Guard of the Führer. It is terrible!"

The future of the NSDAP was bleak. Goebbels wrote in his diary on December 24, "The past is difficult and the future is cloudy and dark. The terrible loneliness overwhelms me with hopelessness. All possibilities and hopes have disappeared." Hitler was even more depressed. "I have given up all hope," he wrote to Frau Wagner after thanking her for a

104. Hitler electioneering with Putzi Hanfstaengl, who was now acting as his foreign press secretary.

105. "Worker, Vote with the Frontline Soldiers, Hitler!"

ARBEITER

WÄHLT DEN FRONTSOLDATEN

HITLER!

106. Winning votes from farmers in East Prussia.

107. Hitler covered Germany by car and plane.

Christmas present. "Nothing will every come of my dreams." He had no hope left; his opponents were too powerful. "As soon as I am sure that everything is lost you know what I'll do, I was always determined to do it. I cannot accept defeat. I will stick to my word and end my life with a bullet."

At this bleak moment Hitler asked Erik Jan Hanussen to cast his horoscope. The famous seer presented a rhymed prediction to the Führer on New Year's Day, 1933. Hitler's power would begin in exactly thirty days.

On January 4 Hitler met secretly with Chancellor von Papen at the home of Baron Kurt von Schröder, one of a group of wealthy men who had recently petitioned Hindenburg to appoint him Chancellor. In the next few weeks there followed other secret meetings and deals with industrialists, military men, and right-wing political leaders. Each group thought it could use Hitler to smash the Reds and control the unions, and so the incredible occurred on January 30: Hitler, who had recently been repudiated by the German electorate, was made Chancellor of the Reich.

A few weeks later, a young Dutch member of "International Communists," a tiny splinter group which opposed Moscow policies, helped Hitler make the first giant step to dictatorship. Marinus van der Lubbe, in a protest against capitalism, set afire the Reichstag. Hitler used this one-man action as an excuse to invoke emergency powers to put down the Red revolution. The Cabinet approved the measure and President von Hindenburg signed the decree without comment.

On March 21 the new Reichstag opened in Potsdam. The ceremony, stage-managed by Goebbels, convinced those present—the military, the Junkers, and the monarchists—that Hitler was subservient to President von Hindenburg and would follow the Prussian ideal.

But two days later, at the first session of the Reichstag, Hitler made it clear that he was subservient to no one. SA and SS men patrolled Berlin's Kroll Opera House, temporary site of the Reichstag, and behind its stage hung a huge swastika flag as a reminder of who was going to be master

108. Hitler's private pilot, Hans Baur (right), with Prince August Wilhelm, the Kaiser's youngest son and an enthusiastic Nazi.

109. Prince August Wilhelm, popularly known as "Auwi," feared the spread of Communism, and his conversion influenced Prince Philip von Hessen, a nephew of the Kaiser and grandson of Queen Victoria, to join in support of Hitler.

of Germany. There was wild applause as Hitler strode up to the podium. He vowed to respect private property, give aid to peasants and the middle class, end unemployment, and promote peace with the world. All he needed was enactment of the Law for Alleviating the Distress of People and Reich. This enabling law would give him overriding although temporary authority in the land, but he made it sound moderate. The Social

Democrats protested but were outvoted 441 to 94, and the Nazis, with outstretched arms, triumphantly sang the "Horst Wessel Song." Democracy was overthrown in the German parliament with scarcely a protest.

This victory brought into the open a number of industrialists who had secretly supported Hitler. Now the steel magnate Krupp openly heiled acquaintances in the street. The bureaucrats stayed at their posts to keep the machinery of government running smoothly. Intellectual and literary figures began espousing the regeneration of Germany through Hitler. It was a revolution, but since on the surface almost bloodless, Germany received it without alarm. There was little resistance because Hitler kept within the law. He had won the temporary confidence of most Germans by an evolutionary policy, only gradually accumulating power in his own hands.

On April 1 Hitler instituted a boycott against the Jews. Storm troopers were posted before the doors of Jewish shops and offices. Jews were removed from all civil service posts and the number of Jews in higher institutions were reduced.

Hitler's personal popularity increased with every speech and public appearance. His birthday on April 20 was widely celebrated.

On May Day, Hitler expounded on the dignity of labor at a rally at Templehof airfield. The next morning the SA and SS, with the help of police, seized union offices throughout the nation. It was the end of organized labor.

The next month he took an even more important step. He outlawed the Social Democratic Party as "hostile to the nation and state." A few days later two other parties voluntarily disbanded, and Hitler proposed to his Cabinet that Germany become a one-party state. The measure passed without dissent. On Bastille Day, July 14, it became law. Germany, like the Soviet Union, was now controlled by a single party and that party by a single man.

The majority of the German people now supported Hitler. A street ruffian a few months earlier, he had been made respectable by the power and prestige of his office. The Führer's growing popularity was shown in the crowds that flocked to his birthplace. Their admiration was growing into a cult. Worshipers even journeyed by bus to honor the birthplace of his mother in Spital. They descended on the farmhouse where the boy Hitler had spent his summers. They climbed on the roof to take pictures, found their way in the courtyard to wash at the wooden trough as if it contained holy water, and chipped pieces from the large stones supporting the barn.

Hitler was so secure in the affections of his own people that he decided to present a similarly affable face to the world. That August he allowed Hanfstaengl, now his foreign press secretary, to publish a book of anti-Hitler caricatures from German and foreign magazines and newspapers. Entitled *Fact vs. Ink*, the jacket showed a good-natured Führer laughing indulgently at his critics. This kind of propanganda appalled

110. Hitler and Hanfstaengl arrive at Oberwiesenfeld, the Munich airport, near which Hitler will address a large crowd gathered in a vast
tent: "He ran the gamut of emotions and a wave of frenzied enthusiasm
swept the mass," Hanfstaengl's son Egon recalled. All shouted and ap-
plauded wildly as a single entity. Eleven-year-old Egon noticed one
incongruous couple—a professor and a charwoman—leaving the tent
"amid the tumultuous acclamation, talking together excitedly, fraternizing in fact."

Goebbels, but Hitler was swayed by Hanfstaengl's reasoning that the
British and Americans would be impressed.

In October Hitler discarded his cautious approach to international
politics. He announced on October 14 that Germany was withdrawing
from the League of Nations and, calling a plebiscite for his action, can-
nily set it for November 12, the day after the anniversary of the Armistice. Hindenburg still regarded Hitler as a house painter and corporal,
but on election eve, he finally identified himself with the Führer and

111. Checking the latest news.

112. A picnic lecture. Magda Goebbels is to Hitler's left.

113. Laughing with his major-domo, Willi Kannenberg.

broadcast an appeal to the nation to "show to the world that we have restored German unity and with God's help shall preserve it." It was an invocation that few patriots could resist, and the next day 95.1 per cent of the electorate approved Hitler's foreign policy. The mandate was so overwhelming that he was able, within weeks, to pass a law unifying party and state. Germany now stood on the threshold of totalitarianism.

114. Occasionally he could spend a few days at his modest villa, Haus Wachenfeld, on the Obersalzberg.

115. Tenant strike in Berlin. Reds join Nazis.

116. Depressed after his 1932 defeat, Hitler tried to find solace that December in his beloved Berchtesgaden.

117. Official proclamation of Hitler as Reichschancellor of Germany, 1933. President von Hindenburg's signature dwarfs Hitler's, and for several months Hitler remained in Hindenburg's shadow.

118. United States Nazis in the Yorkville section of New York City celebrate Hitler's great victory.

119. Hitler's Cabinet. From left to right, Seldt, Guertner, Goebbels, Elz von Rubenach, Hitler, Göring, Blomberg, Frick, Neurath, Schacht, Schwerin von Krosigk, unknown, Papen.

120. Hitler makes his first speech to the nation. February 1, 1933.

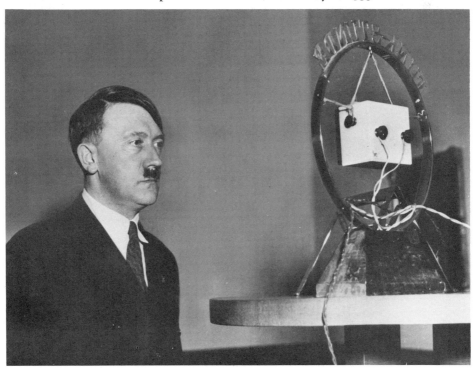

121. The Reichstag fire.

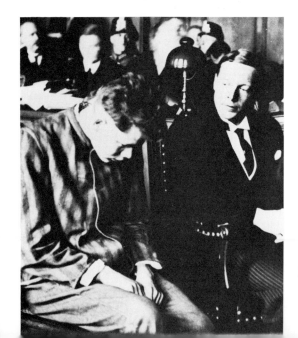

122. Marinus van der Lubbe on trial.

123. Hitler is still concerned as he listens to the results of the March 5 election. The Nazis received only 43.9 per cent of the votes, and it took those of his nationalist allies to give him a bare majority in the parliament.

124. Hindenburg and son drive to the Potsdam garrison church.

125. Blomberg, Hindenburg, Hitler, Göring, and Hindenburg's son, Oskar, honor the war dead a few days before the Potsdam ceremony.

126. Chancellor Hitler plays a secondary role during an address by Hindenburg at a youth convention in the Lustgarten in May.

127. Anti-Jewish action: "Germans! Don't buy from Jews!"

128. Hitler also feared that he was part Jewish and in 1931 had sent his private lawyer, Hans Frank, into Austria to check. Frank returned with the disconcerting report that Hitler's grandmother Schicklgruber had been "working for a Jewish family named Frankenberger when she gave birth to her son. And Frankenberger—this happened in the late 1830s—paid a paternity allowance on behalf of his nineteen-year-old son from the birth of the Schicklgruber woman's son until he was 14." Postwar research has tended to prove that there was little chance of Hitler's having had Jewish ancestry, but at the time he was badly shaken by Frank's report and lied to him in an attempt to discredit it.

129. Hitler honored with Goethe and Henry Ford—all nonsmokers, nondrinkers.

130. April 20, 1933: Happy Birthday!

131–132. Hands reach for the Führer.

133. On May 10 students, organized by Goebbels (once a novelist himself),
burned more than 20,000 "subversive" books, including those of Remarque,
Mann, Brecht, Hemingway, Proust, Zola, Upton Sinclair, and H. G. Wells. "The
soul of the German people," Goebbels told the students, "can now express itself."

134. That summer Nazi mass marriages were staged: Fifty couples, all belong-
ing to the militant "German Christian" group, parade through Berlin.

135. Braunau birthplace with banners.

136. Spital: "It was like a country fair," recalled a Hitler relative. "They painted swastikas on the cows and would parade around singing Hitler songs."

138. From a French language paper in Cairo, May 1933: "If strangers accuse us of barbarity, we will give you another turn of the screw!"

137. From *Der Wahr Jacob*, Berlin, November 1931: "They call Mr. Hitler the drummer. Drumming has long been known as the most primitive way to make oneself understood."

139. The year ends in triumph at Munich. Hitler and the Old Fighters follow the Blood Flag in a re-enactment of the march in 1923.

140. A Brownshirt points to the Führer's pistol shot in the ceiling.

141. Sister Pia, a heroine of the Putsch.

SIX

Year of Crises

1934

To counter a proposed alliance in the spring of 1934 between France and the Soviet Union, Hitler sought a strong ally. In June he set out for Italy to woo Mussolini—but with some reluctance. Hitler had been a hero-worshiper of Il Duce since his march on Rome. This, in fact, had inspired him to stage a march of his own which became the disastrous Beer Hall Putsch. While in prison in 1924, however, he had sent Göring to Italy to get a two-million-lire loan from the Fascists. But Mussolini had turned him down peremptorily on the grounds that the NSDAP was a minor party, and Hitler was still resentful.

Their historic meeting was doomed from the start. When Hitler stepped out of his plane at Lido airfield on June 14, he looked like a struggling salesman in his worn trench coat and blue serge suit. He was met by a Duce dressed in black shirt, jack boots, and glittering gold braid. Hitler acted like a schoolboy and didn't even know what to do with his fedora.

Their first conversation was a disaster, with Mussolini dominating the talk. Nor was Hitler favorably impressed by the Italian Navy when he saw sailors' washing flying from the masts. At their final meeting on a golf course, Il Duce was openly bored by Hitler's talk and the Führer left Venice stung by the realization that he had been not only snubbed by Mussolini but outmaneuvered diplomatically.

Upon Hitler's return home he was presented with a major crisis, the so-called Röhm Putsch. For some months Ernst Röhm, leader of the Brownshirts, had been demanding a military role for his men. The Army, naturally, opposed it. Secretly enemies of Röhm in the SS were already involved in a plot to destroy him. Himmler was then joined in the plot by Göring and Goebbels, both of whom were jealous of Röhm's growing power. They convinced Hitler that Röhm was about to stage a revolution, and so a bloody purge began, with many old scores being settled that had nothing to do with the so-called Putsch. Perhaps two hundred

men—the exact number will never be known—were executed. Ironically, Röhm had no intention of revolting, and many of those murdered, including Gregor Strasser and Generals Kurt von Schleicher and Kurt von Bredow, had no connection with Röhm. The Nazis later made much of Röhm's homosexuality, but Hitler had known of this for several years. A man's private life was his own, he said. "But God help Röhm if he abuses young boys! Then he must go!"

The purge cost the NSDAP many of its most ardent members, the idealists of the SA. They were convinced that Röhm had merely attempted to bring Hitler back to the old ideals of National Socialism. "And here it was," recalled one of these men, "that Hitler really made his first true enemies, enemies in his own camp. For me and my friends, Hitler as a human being was finished."

Another crisis came a month later when Chancellor Engelbert Dollfuss of Austria was assassinated by Austrian Nazis. It was charged that Hitler had inspired the local Nazis, and he had to send Papen to Vienna to smooth over the affair. The shock of the Röhm purge, followed so quickly by that of the Dollfuss murder, affected Hindenburg. His health declined rapidly and soon he was confined to his bed. Now there was a crisis of a different nature. Who would succeed Hindenburg? Hitler made several trips to the Field Marshal's estate.

On August 2 Hitler's Cabinet passed a law combining the offices of President and Chancellor to become effective on the death of Hindenburg. Within the hour, he died on his spartan iron cot with the last words: "My Kaiser, my Fatherland." As a result of Hitler's legal maneuver, he now carried the title of Führer and Reich Chancellor. This meant he was also supreme commander of the armed forces. His first act was to summon General Werner von Blomberg, Minister of Defense, and the three commanders in chief of the armed forces. Hitler asked them to take an oath swearing before God to give their "unconditional obedience to Adolf Hitler, Führer of the Reich and its people, Supreme Commander of the Armed Forces." Before the end of the day, every officer and man in the land took the same oath of personal fealty. It was unprecedented, but there is no record of any officer having protested or even questioning the unique wording.

Twelve days later, the German people went to the polls, and almost 90 per cent voted their approval of Adolf Hitler as Hindenburg's successor.

That September Hitler's position was solidified at the Nuremberg Party Day Congress. He had selected Albert Speer as stage manager and Leni Riefenstahl as film maker. She accepted the assignment reluctantly on the grounds that she didn't know the difference between the SA and the SS. "That is why I want you to do it,'" said Hitler. "That will give it a fresh approach." She devised shots from planes, cranes, roller skates, and a tiny elevator attached to the tallest flagpole.

As the phenomenon of the Nuremberg rallies suggests, Hitler's appeal

was, for many Germans, more than just political. "He is," Dr. Carl Jung observed at a later point in Hitler's life, "the first man to tell every German what he has been thinking and feeling all along in his unconscious about German fate, especially since the defeat in the World War, and the one characteristic which colors every German soul is the typical German inferiority complex, the complex of the younger brother, of the one who is always a bit late to the feast. Hitler's power is not political; it is *magic*." Of Hitler Freud said: "You cannot tell what a madman will do."

142. Hours after his humiliating visit with Mussolini, Hitler received another blow. Vice-chancellor von Papen delivered a speech at Marburg vigorously attacking Goebbels and the controlled press and then urging Hitler to break with Röhm and his so-called Second Revolution. Papen's assistant, who wrote the speech, will be murdered during the Röhm Putsch.

143. Hitler and Röhm, the closest of comrades, at the last Party Day.

144–45. Röhm at his Munich home. His mother agreed to this invasion of her privacy. "It is for my son," she said, "that the world may know him as he really is." To this day, Röhm's brother and his sister-in-law do not believe he was a homosexual.

146. The plot against Röhm had begun. Here he is flanked by Himmler, who initiated the scheme, and Hitler, who is not yet aware of it.

147. Goebbels (smiling, right) had entered the conspiracy.

148. Although by this time Hitler was under anti-Röhm pressure from all sides, Röhm still did not seem greatly worried about the rumors of a Göring-Goebbels-Himmler plot against him. "He had some feeling that there was something wrong," his sister-in-law recalled, "but still did not take it seriously. He never had any doubts whatsoever about Hitler."

149. Assured that Röhm is a traitor (he actually was not), Hitler sent Sepp Dietrich, commander of his SS bodyguard, to Bad Wiessee, a lake resort south of Munich, to arrest Röhm and his group.

150. A little later Hitler decided to handle the matter in person. Here he is being briefed at the Munich airport. He would soon drive to Bad Wiessee and supervise the arrests.

151. General Blomberg (right) with Field Marshal August von Mackensen, hero of the Great War, who was one of the few officers to openly protest the assassinations of Generals von Schleicher and Bredow.

152. Dollfuss reviewing monarchist paratroops the year before his assassination.

153. One of the final meetings between Hitler and the failing Hindenburg.

154. August 1, 1934: Hitler's last visit to the Hindenburg estate. Oskar von Hindenburg escorted him to his father's bedside, telling his father that the Chancellor had one or two important matters to discuss. Hindenburg opened his eyes, stared at Hitler, and clamped his mouth shut.

155. The next day Hindenburg died.

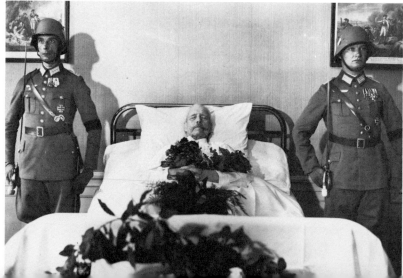

156. Hindenburg had wished to be buried near his estate, but Hitler insisted that burial take place at Tannenberg, scene of the Marshal's greatest triumph. Here Speer is making plans for a state funeral at the Tannenberg monument.

157. The body was placed on a catafalque in the center of the monument. Fires flamed from the sixty-foot towers. It reminded French Ambassador François-Poncet of a castle built by the Teutonic Knights.

158. Hitler relaxes with Eva (blonde) at Chiemsee, a lake not far from Berchtesgaden.

159. Eva rows.

160. By the fall of 1934 the Hitler movement had won wide acceptance. Here a Protestant rector blesses Nazi flags.

161. Hess, Speer, and Hitler.

162–63. Hitler with Leni Riefenstahl, and with Viktor Lutze who had succeeded Röhm as head of the SA.

164. Mock battle.

165. Hitler and Baldur von Schirach, the Reich youth leader, review the Hitler Jugend.

166. The SA and SS parade together. Months earlier, during the Röhm Putsch, the two groups had been fighting.

168. Aerial view of rally.

167. Speer's dramatic lighting effects.

SEVEN

War in Masquerade

1935–1936

The time had come at last to regain lost territories, and the first victory came on January 13, 1935, when the people of the Saar voted overwhelmingly to return to the Reich. On March 16 Hitler shocked the world by proclaiming universal military service and raising the peacetime army to 300,000 men. Hitler claimed that his intentions were purely defensive and his main enemy Communist Russia. A few days later he met with Sir John Simon and Anthony Eden to discuss disarmament. In June the British not only allowed Germany to fix her naval tonnage at 35 per cent of their own fleet but conceded a 45 per cent ratio for submarines. It was a notable diplomatic victory for Ribbentrop and Hitler.

Consequently Hitler's popularity at home that year increased.

The following year was even more successful. On March 7, 1936, against the advice of his generals, Hitler sent his troops into the demilitarized zone of the Rhineland. They had secret orders to retreat if challenged by French troops. But there was no resistance. Gemany had another bloodless victory, and no head of state in the world now enjoyed such popularity.

Two inner circles had formed around Hitler—one composed of top associates like Goebbels, Göring, Hess (and their wives), and another on a more personal level: the chauffeurs, secretaries, servants, and other intimates. This innermost circle, which included such disparate members as an architect, Speer, and a pilot, Hans Baur, also took in some of the younger military adjutants. A few belonged to both circles, most notably Martin Bormann, who had been working for Hess since the early days and now, as his representative in Berlin, was given the opportunity of assiduously devoting himself to the daily needs of the Führer. Although unknown to most Germans, the indefatigable Bormann had become Hitler's shadow.

Preoccupation with the international scene gave Hitler little time for his mistress, Eva Braun. In 1935 she became so despondent she swal-

169. Hitler visits Saarbrücken on March 1, 1935.

lowed twenty pills in a second attempt at suicide. She was found in a coma by her sister, Ilse, and saved. After this Hitler was much more attentive and brought Eva to his chalet on the Obersalzberg so often that his half sister, Angela, the housekeeper of Haus Wachenfeld, became incensed. Angela referred to Eva as *die blöde Kuh* (the stupid cow) and refused to shake hands. The relationship between Angela and Hitler became so strained that she gave up her post as housekeeper to get married. So, by 1936, Eva had become the undisputed mistress of Haus Wachenfeld, which was already undergoing total reconstruction. As official summer residence it had to be enlarged to accommodate high-level diplomatic negotiations—and provide Eva with a bedroom, boudoir, and bath adjoining Hitler's own room and studio. It also had a new name, the Berghof.

Hitler welcomed many famous visitors to the Berghof and to the Chancellery, but Eva would be confined to her quarters since their liaison was still a secret. She longed to meet Lloyd George, Admiral Horthy of Hungary, King Carol of Romania, the Aga Khan, and such notables and yet was forced to stay in her room like a child. She was particularly disturbed, she confided to friends, when Hitler refused her pleas to meet the Duchess of Windsor, since the two women, she thought, had so much in common. She did console herself with the thrill of knowing that the great of the world were coming from all over to honor her lover. This knowledge made her "Back Street" existence endurable.

Overleaf: 170. Saar demonstration.

171. Disarmament conference. Afterward Hitler and Eden talked over their war-time experiences. They had fought opposite each other and together drew a map of the battle lines on the back of a dinner card.

172. Now when Hitler talks nearly all Germany seems to be listening: Goebbels, Milch, Darre, Elz von Rubenach, Blomberg, Guertner, and Seldt at the Reichstag.

173. Berliners gathered near outdoor radio speakers.

174. The Ribbentrops returning from the polls. In early 1936 Hitler had campaigned throughout Germany on the question of his seizure of the Rhineland. "What I have done," he told one audience, "I did according to my conscience, and to the best of my knowledge, filled with concern for my people, realizing the necessity of protecting its honor, in order to lead it again to a position of honor in this world. And should unnecessary sorrow or suffering ever come to my people because of my actions, then I beseech the Almighty God to punish me."

A week later the people went to the polls: 98.8 per cent voted for Hitler. (The poster to the right of the Ribbentrops reads: "The Führer gave us freedom and honor!")

175. French troops evacuating from the Rhineland.

THE HESSES

176. Bormann at wheel with Frau Hess; Hess on jump seat; in back Professor Karl Haushofer, the geopolitician, and Hildegard Fath, Hess's secretary.

177. Hess with his wife on a skiing holiday in the mid-1930s. He usually kept a stiff upper lip—to cover his buck teeth.

178. Athlete Hess takes off.

179. Professor Haushofer, Hess's mentor and friend. Frau Haushofer was Jewish and Hess protected her. Later one of the Haushofer sons became involved in the plot against Hitler and was executed.

180. Hess has just won the hazardous air race around the Zugspitze, Germany's highest peak, near Garmsich.

THE GOEBBELSES

181. One-pot dinner with the Führer.

182. Goebbels and his stepson.

183. Hitler greets his half sister, Angela, Magda Goebbels, and her son, Harald, by a previous marriage.

184. The Goebbelses with Winifred Wagner at Bayreuth.

THE GÖRINGS

185. Göring soon after the Great War.

186. Second marriage, to actress Emmy Sonnemann, in 1935. An irreverent flying comrade has just released two storks over the Evangelical Cathedral in Berlin. As the bride and groom leave the church a military band thunders out the march from *Lohengrin*.

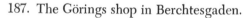

187. The Görings shop in Berchtesgaden.

188. Karin Hall, Göring's country estate near Berlin, was named after his first wife, Carin, but misspelled.

189. Rare photo of a pornographic table reported to be Göring's.

190. Göring on the Obersalzberg with a neighbor.

191. His chalet is in the background. Nearby were those of Hitler and Bormann.

192. Easter, 1935.

193. Eva at the Niklaus Ball, December 1935.

194. Eva at the winter Olympic games in Garmisch, 1936.

195. Olympic hockey game. During the crucial game Hitler became too nervous to stay until the end and had to have someone give him a brief account later.

196. Hitler bought Eva a love nest in Munich after her second suicide attempt.

197. At her new home.

198. Mother Braun and daughters.

199. The Berghof, exterior.

200. Hitler's architectural sketch for the comprehensive alterations which would transform his Obersalzberg villa, Haus Wachenfeld (see photo ✳114), into "the Berghof." The traditional pitched roof design was part of his architectural credo: "the house with the flat roof," he wrote in 1924, "is oriental—oriental is Jewish—Jewish is bolshevistic."

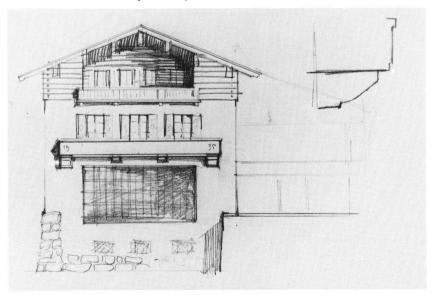

201. The Berghof, interior.

202. Eva's bedroom at the Berghof.

203. The passageway leading to it.

OBERSALZBERG VOR DER ZERSTÖRUNG

204. View of the Obersalzberg at the height of its development. Not shown are the homes of Bormann and Göring, which were behind the photographer's vantage point. The numbered buildings are identified as follows: "1. Post office off-limit area. 2. Gardening ground. 3. Quarter of drivers. 4. Grand garage. 5. House with gateway to 'off-limit area.' 6. Barrack, officers, and kitchen apart-

205–6. A view of the Berghof showing in the foreground the walkway Hitler would daily take down to the teahouse, a round stone building below.

ments. 7. Barrack, drill hall of the bodyguard. 8. Barrack square, with underground shooting ranges. 9. Barrack, dwelling house. 10. Hotel 'Platterhof.' 11. Dwelling house for the personnel of the Hotel Platterhof. 12. Intendancy of Obersalzberg. 13. Studio for architectural projecting. 14. Kindergarten house. 15. 'Berghof.' 16. Security Service of the Reich and Gestapo."

207–8. Hitler reading at the teahouse and dozing with Eva. Here he would drink apple-peel tea while Eva talked of plays and movies; the general conversation would usually be gay and superficial but occasionally Hitler would propagandize for vegetarianism, decry smoking and drinking, or expound the dangers of women using polluted make-up.

209–12. Five miles from the Berghof by a winding road, much of it blasted out of rock, was Hitler's mile-high mountain teahouse atop the Kehlstein. Visitors would drive up this road to an underground passage dug into the peak. At the end of the corridor was a copper-lined elevator, its shaft hacked out of solid rock. After a ride of about four hundred feet, it opened onto a gallery of Roman pillars. Beyond was an immense glassed-in circular hall. Great logs were burning in a huge open fireplace. On all sides extended such an immense panorama of mountains that visitors were given a sensation of being suspended in space.

213–14. Hitler and Eva with guests at the Kehlstein. After several visits the fantastic setting began to pall on Hitler because of its grandiosity.

215. Receiving Lloyd George.

216. The Lindberghs visit Germany, here escorted by General Erhard Milch, who was to become a Luftwaffe field marshal. Lindbergh was impressed by what he saw of German air strength. Later Göring presented him with the German Eagle, one of the highest German decorations, "by order of der Führer." In early 1939 Lindbergh wrote in his diary that Hitler held the future of Europe in his hands. "Much as I disapprove of many things Germany has done, I believe she has pursued the only consistent policy in Europe in recent years."

217. Hitler reminisces about the old days with a former war comrade, Ignaz Westenkirchner, and his family, while Amann, also a war comrade, and Hanfstaengl listen in.

218. Max Schmeling became a hero to Hitler in 1936 when he knocked out Joe Louis in the twelfth round—thus demonstrating the supremacy of the white race. Two years later Louis knocked out Schmeling in one round.

219. Hitler greets German Olympic stars.

220. The achievements of 1936 were highlighted for Hitler by the triumphant summer Olympics. Three Americans have just swept the decathlon but the crowd gives an enthusiastic "Heil, Hitler." Germany won the most gold medals (thirty-three), as well as the most silver and bronze, surprising everyone by beating the second-place Americans by fifty-seven points. Leni Riefenstahl recorded the victory in a two-part documentary, but most important for the Nazi regime were the favorable impressions of Hitler's Germany taken home by many of the visitors.

EIGHT

Tomorrow the World

1937–1938

On January 30, 1937, Hitler addressed the Reichstag to commemorate his first four years in office. To the German people his achievements truly seemed impressive. He had defied tradition to expand production and curb unemployment. He was changing the face of the land with a network of *Autobahnen,* as well as developing a "People's Car" so compact and inexpensive that the average German could afford it. He envisaged other innovations for the future. In large cities there would be automated underground parking, traffic-free centers, parks and green areas, and strict pollution control. Antipollution devices were already installed in some factories in the Ruhr, and new plants were required to construct preventive devices to avoid pollution of the waters.

Unlike most Germans, though, Hitler had no use for the Zeppelin. He said it was against nature: "She has provided no bird with any sort of balloon, as she has done in the case of the fish. As far as I myself am concerned, I shall never consent to go up in a dirigible."

The welfare and training of youth were also given priority: Little children were taught absolute loyalty to the Führer and Greater Reich; older ones were required to attend work camps, with the rich laboring next to the poor.

While preparing the nation mentally and physically for the task of bringing Germany to "glory and prosperity," Hitler had managed in four years to raise the health standards to such a degree that many foreigners were impressed. Working conditions were also improved with more windows, less crowding, and better washrooms. Never before had the worker enjoyed such privileges. The "Strength Through Joy" program initiated by Robert Ley's Labor Front provided subsidized concerts, theater preformances, dances, films, adult education courses, and subsidized tourism. Now the humblest laborer and his family could travel aboard luxury liners for undreamed-of holidays.

Hitler's greatest achievement was perhaps his unification of the Ger-

221. Hitler at the auto show.

222. Hitler digs the first shovel of dirt for the *Autobahn* between Frankfurt and Darmstadt.

man nation, but this had been accomplished at the cost of civil liberties. This was not the only price paid for Hitler's program: He had lifted the nation out of depression by speeding up rearmament and thus forced Germany into a potentially disastrous situation.

Even so, if Hitler had died in 1937 he would have gone down as a great figure in German history. Throughout Europe he had millions of admirers. Gertrude Stein thought Hitler should get the Nobel Peace Prize. Shaw defended him, and so did Sven Hedin, the Swedish ex-

223. Little girls learning Nazi salute.

Mein Führer!

(Das Kind spricht:)

Ich kenne dich wohl und habe dich lieb
                wie Vater und Mutter.
Ich will dir immer gehorsam sein
                wie Vater und Mutter.
Und wenn ich groß bin, helfe ich dir
                wie Vater und Mutter,
Und freuen sollst du dich an mir
                wie Vater und Mutter!

224. From a Nazi children's coloring book: "My Führer!/I know you well and love you/like father and mother. I will always obey you/like father and mother. And when I grow up I will help you/like father and mother,/And you will be proud of me/like father and mother!"

225. Everyone works for the Third Reich. A labor camp for Hitler maidens who come from every walk of life.

226. Village children see movies for the first time at a traveling cinema theater sponsored by the "Strength Through Joy" program.

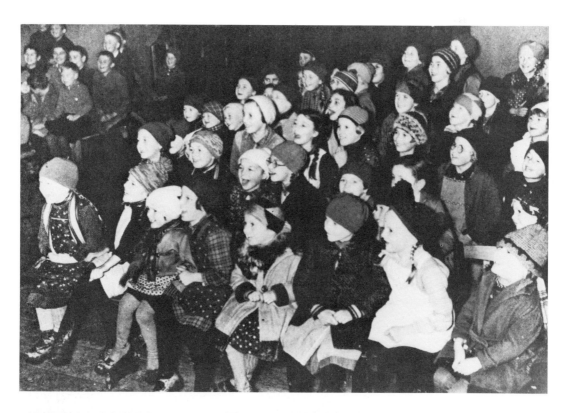

227. Léon Degrelle, head of the Belgian Rexist movement. He regarded himself as the spiritual son of Hitler.

plorer. Hitler also, by example, stimulated the growth of movements similiar to his own throughout Europe and even in the United States.

The people of Germany continued to pay homage and flocked to the Berghof whenever it was rumored that Hitler would be there.

On the brink of dictatorship, Hitler remained the artist and architect. Art and politics were to him inseparable. The architect he revered was Professor Paul Ludwig Troost. Perhaps his most memorable project for

228. A member of Sir Oswald Mosley's Blackshirts with the Brownshirts.

229–30. Hitler with some of the many admirers who came to see him at the Berghof, in candid photos taken by his chauffeur, Eric Kempka.

Hitler was a modern art museum for Munich, the Haus der Deutschen Kunst. Professor Troost died soon after the cornerstone was laid but his young widow carried on his work, and every time Hitler came to Munich he would visit her studio. A lady with a mind of her own, she expressed it forthrightly. But, to the surprise of his aides, Hitler did not resent Frau Troost's candor—except on one memorable occasion. For the grand opening of the Haus der Deutschen Kunst in the summer of 1937 an ambitious exhibition of German art was scheduled. The judges, including Frau Troost, selected a good many excellent modern paintings which Hitler considered degenerate. He and Frau Troost consequently had a violent argument at the museum just before opening day. She refused to back down. "And since you can't approve our selection and have a com-

231. To the right, Hitler greets an admirer gallantly. The two colorfully dressed youths, left, are apprentice carpenters from Hamburg.

pletely different opinion," she said, "I resign this moment as a member of the jury." They parted coolly but a few weeks later Hitler was back at the Troost studio as if nothing had happened.

On January 12, 1938, Field Marshal von Blomberg, the Minister of Defense, married his typist, with Göring and Hitler as witnesses. No sooner had the couple left on a honeymoon than it was revealed that the young Frau von Blomberg had been a prostitute. Hitler expressed shock and exclaimed, "If a German field marshal marries a whore, then anything in this world is possible!" Blomberg's fellow officers also demanded his resignation and it was expected that General Werner von Fritsch would succeed him. Then it was charged that Fritsch had been involved in homosexual acts. Hitler promptly ordered a full Gestapo investigation of the scandal and chose as the new army commander in chief General Walther von Brauchitsch, an open admirer although not a Nazi Party member.

With a more compliant Minister of Defense, Hitler summoned his Cabinet on February 4. He announced that he was reorganizing the Wehrmacht and had taken over personal command of the entire armed forces. It was the last time the Cabinet would ever meet and it was fitting that its members merely sat and approved. Just before midnight the German people were informed by radio of this momentous decision. They also learned that Blomberg and Fritsch had resigned, sixteen high-ranking

232. The wedding of Eva's friend Marion Schönemann to Herr Theissen, at the Berghof, August 1937. Kneeling near groom, Gretl Braun, Eva's sister. Standing, left to right, Heinrich Hoffmann, Frau Honni Morell, Erma Hoffmann, Eva Braun, Frau Dreesen (her husband owned the Hotel Dreesen), Dr. Morell, Herta Schneider (Eva's best friend), two unidentified men, and Hitler.

234. On May 7, 1937, Hitler's apprehensions became a reality. The *Hindenburg's* explosion, which could have been sabotage, ended the epoch of giant rigid dirigibles.

generals had been dismissed, and that Hermann Göring had been promoted to Luftwaffe field marshal. The next morning the headlines of Hitler's newspaper, the *Völkischer Beobachter*, read:

STRONGEST CONCENTRATION OF ALL POWERS IN THE FÜHRER'S HANDS!

At last Hitler was the supreme dictator of the German Reich. Overriding objections of his generals, he marched into Austria.

Hitler's next goal was Czechoslovakia, which he regarded as a dagger aimed at the heart of Germany. All he needed was an excuse to invade and he had a ready-made one, Czechoslovakia's German minority. The 3,500,000 million people of the Sudetenland, inspired by the absorption of Austria, were now demanding a similar *Anschluss*. But Hitler was restrained by fear that France, England, and perhaps Russia would resist any invasion. Before facing such odds he wanted the blessing of his only ally, Italy, and on May 2, set out to get it.

101

233. The *Hindenburg* flies over the 1936 Nuremberg Party Day.

235. Frau Troost, Goebbels, Hitler, and Hess at the opening ceremonies for the Haus der Deutschen Kunst.

Hitler's threat to Czechoslovakia finally aroused England to action. Prime Minister Chamberlain flew to Munich to confer with Hitler at the Berghof and later in Bad Godesberg.

The problem was finally solved at the famous Munich Conference between Chamberlain, Hitler, Mussolini, and French Premier Daladier six days later. The Sudetenland was to be evacuated by the Czechs in four stages to begin on October 1.

The year ended with a violent attack on Jews—Crystal Night. It was sparked by the shooting of a minor German Foreign Office official in Paris on November 7, by a young Jew, Herschel Grynszpan, whose parents had been deported from Germany to Poland. He had gone to the embassy to assassinate the ambassador only to be sidetracked by Counselor Ernest von Rath. Himself an enemy of anti-Semites, Rath was being investigated by the Gestapo but it was he who took the bullets intended for his superior.

Rath's death was used as an excuse to ransack Jewish shops, burn synagogues, and commit murder. By official account thirty-six Jews were killed and another thirty-six seriously injured. But the figures, SS General Reinhard Heydrich himself admitted, "must have been exceeded considerably."

236. The "Eternal Jew" Exhibition also opened that year in Munich.

237. Arno Breker, one of Europe's leading sculptors, working on a bust of Speer in the style Hitler preferred.

238. "Anmut," by Breker.

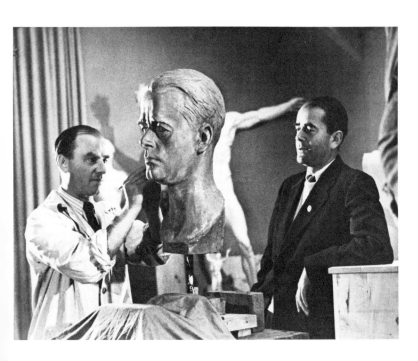

NAZI ARCHITECTURE

239. Speer's model of Berlin's proposed new center: Arch of Triumph with Great Domed Hall at far end.

240. Hitler dreamed of similar structures in his youth and made this sketch of a Great Domed Hall in 1925.

241. Hitler's sketch of a triumphal arch with domed hall visible in background to the left, also made in 1925.

242. March 1937 Hitler design for the pedestal to a monument.

243. November 1942 Hitler sketch for a monument to composer Anton Bruckner in Linz.

244. The same year: sketch for bridge over the Elbe in Hamburg.

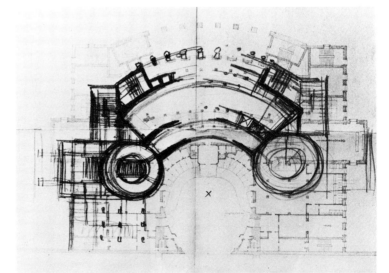

245. Rough Hitler sketch for a theater interior in Linz superimposed on plan.

246. The Guests of the Führer. Eva between Hitler and the Bormanns.

247. Hitler's thank-you note for holiday greetings.

248. Hitler, Blomberg, and Fritsch. The end is near for both generals.

250. Austrian Prime Minister von Schuschnigg tried in vain to stop the Nazi take-over.

249. Blomberg, Hitler, Göring, and Goebbels at the horse show.

251. Enthusiastic crowds greet the German troops as they enter Vienna on March 14, 1938.

253. In Italy Hitler got what he came for: assurance that Czechoslovakia was not at all important to Mussolini, and tacit approval for Hitler's expansionist plans.

252. On March 16 Hitler gets a triumphant welcome in Berlin.

254. Eva celebrates Fasching that year with her mother (center) and sisters. She and Hitler were now living comfortably as man and wife, and with her position more stable, Eva could enjoy herself when he was busy with politics.

255. Eva en route to Italy with Frau Dreesen, wife of the owner of one of Hitler's favorite hotels, the Hotel Dreesen in Bad Godesberg.

256. On the bar at Tegernsee, where Röhm was arrested during the 1934 Putsch.

257. And relaxing during an office party at Hoffmann's photographic studio, where she had resumed work. It is doubtful whether Hitler would have approved her position on the floor, and certainly not her smoking. Not long after this he gave her an ultimatum: "Either give up smoking or me." She chose to give up smoking. To others in the family circle he had a standing offer of a gold watch for anyone who renounced tobacco.

258. At the Berghof, Goebbels entertains Eva, Speer, and others.

259. Candid shot of Hitler on the veranda of the Berghof.

260. Hitler and ordnance officer Max Wünsche visit a girls' school in Berchtesgaden.

261. Hitler with the Speer children. Eva takes a picture.

262. In Berlin Hitler attends the baptism of Edda Göring.

263. Hitler standing in limousine outside the Rheinhotel Dreesen.

264. Inside he assures Chamberlain that the Czech problem is "the last territorial demand" which he has to make in Europe.

265. The Führer is obviously in good spirits as he bids good-by to his guest—he has won the Sudetenland. Chamberlain was also pleased. Arriving in England, he announced that he had achieved peace with honor. "I believe it is peace in our time."

266. "The Game of Princes."

267. German troops enter the Sudetenland on October 1.

268. Two days later Hitler makes his triumphal entry.

269. Funeral service for diplomat Ernst von Rath, with Hitler in attendance.

270. That November, Hitler saying farewell to another guest. The year 1938 has been one of diplomatic triumph for him—diplomacy backed with the threat of overwhelming force.

NINE

The Road to War

1939–1940

The year 1939 began peacefully enough with the celebration of an ancient Teutonic ceremony at the Berghof. Molten lead was poured into a small basin of water and the shape it assumed supposedly determined the future.

On January 30 Hitler publicly hinted at his secret plan to exterminate Europe's Jews. "Today I shall act the prophet once again," he told the Reichstag. "If international Jewry inside and outside of Europe should succeed in thrusting the nations into a world war once again, then the result will not be the Bolshevization of the earth and with it the victory of Jewry, it will be the *annihilation of the Jewish race in Europe.*" Witnesses noted "long and vigorous applause."

That March Hitler made his move to take the rest of Czechoslovakia. First he summoned Monsignor Josef Tiso of Slovakia to Berlin and bullied him. The next evening, March 14, he called in President Emil Hacha of Czechoslovakia and also threatened him into submission. During the ordeal Hacha fainted. On March 15 Hitler occupied Czechoslovakia without bloodshed.

A week later came another conquest, with Hitler 'persuading' the Lithuanians to sign over to him the district of Memel.

Foreign diplomats correctly assumed Hitler's next target would be Poland. Soon, Polish Foreign Minister Josef Beck visited the Berghof. If he feared being browbeaten like Tiso, Hacha, and Austrian Chancellor Kurt von Schuschnigg, he was pleasantly surprised. There were no threats, only inducements. But Beck, as diplomatically as possible, refused even to consider the return of Danzig. Poland's plucky stand was rewarded that spring by a startling offer of military assistance from London in case of Nazi aggression. Beck accepted "without hesitation," and at last England was united and committed. There would be no more appeasement.

Hitler spent much of that summer at the Berghof, relaxing in preparation for his next political move. Eva was always nearby and took many pictures of the Führer and his visitors.

271. Pouring lead to read the future. "Hitler," recalled Ilse Braun, "did not seem satisfied with the results, for afterwards he sat down in an armchair, gazing dejectedly at the fire, and hardly spoke for the rest of the evening."

Hitler had agreed to let Stalin have the eastern half of Poland, which meant that the Soviet Union at least had been neutralized. Hitler was elated. Now he was free to proceed. Late that night he led his entourage onto the Berghof terrace. The sky in the north blazed wtih all the colors of the rainbow. It reminded Speer of the last act of *Götterdämmerung*. Hitler abruptly turned to his Luftwaffe adjutant. "Looks like a great deal of blood," he said. "This time we won't bring it off without violence."

On the morning of September 1, German artillery fire crashed down along the Polish-German border, followed by a massive attack of Nazi infantry and tanks. There was no formal declaration of war until late that morning when Hitler addressed the Reichstag at the Kroll Opera House. "I carry on this fight," he said, "no matter against whom, until the safety of the Reich and its rights are secured."

The Polish defenders were overwhelmed by a new form of warfare:

272. President Hacha of Czechoslovakia.

273. On March 15 the Nazis occupied Czechoslovakia without bloodshed.

Blitzkrieg! Lightning war. By the morning of September 5 the Polish Air Force was destroyed, and two days later most of Poland's thirty-five divisions were either routed or had surrendered.

Once Poland was conquered, Hitler began transforming it into a massive killing ground. He had already ordered Jews from the Reich massed in specific Polish cities having good rail connections. Object: "final solution, which will take some time," as Heydrich, head of the dreaded Security Service, told SS commanders on September 21. He was talking of the extermination of the Jews, already an open secret among many high-ranking party officials. These grisly preparations were augmented by a "house cleaning" of Polish intelligentsia, clergy, and nobility by five murder squads known as *Einsatzgruppen* (Special Action Groups). By midautumn of 1939, 3,500 intelligentsia were liquidated. "It is only in this manner," Hitler explained, "that we can acquire the vital territory which we need. After all, who today remembers the extermination of the Armenians." In addition to the urban terror campaign was the ruthless expulsion of 1,200,000 ordinary Poles from their ancestral homes; many of these people lost their lives in the resettlement from exposure to zero weather.

On the last day of September, Hitler went to Berlin and, in a speech at the Sport Palace, reminded the audience of his threat of annihilation to Jews if they should "start another" world war. "Some time ago the Jews laughed about my prophecies in Germany, too. I do not know whether they are still laughing today or whether they have stopped laughing already. I can only assure you even now; they will stop laughing everywhere. And I shall be proved right with these prophecies as well."

In November Hitler again returned to Munich for the annual commemoration of the Beer Hall Putsch. As he addressed the audience a

118

274. On March 24 Hitler made his triumphal entry into Memel.

bomb, hidden in a column just behind him, was ticking away. That afternoon Frau Troost had warned him of possible assassination and he decided to take an earlier train. Hitler hurried his speech and left the hall ahead of time. Exactly eight minutes later the bomb exploded, killing seven and wounding sixty-three, including Eva Braun's father. Eva arrived at the station just as the Führer's train was leaving and found an air of carefree gaiety.

On March 18, 1940, Hitler met Mussolini at the Brenner Pass in a snowstorm. He had come, he said, "simply to explain the situation" so Il Duce could make his own decision. Without hesitation Mussolini agreed to join Hitler in his war against the West. It began on April 7 with attacks on Denmark and Norway.

Now the stage was set for the main invasion. On the morning of May 10 German troops flooded across the Belgian, Holland, and Luxembourg borders. England and France, despite warnings, were caught by surprise.

275. Hitler was convinced that a show of power would give him Poland without war. The quixotic Mussolini was persuaded to conclude the so-called Pact of Steel, and his son-in-law, Count Galeazzo Ciano, came to Berlin to sign it. Foreign Minister Ribbentrop sits to the right.

276. Eva, the self-styled "Rolleiflex Girl."

Hitler's unprecedented victory was followed by a diplomatic success, the signing of the Tripartite Pact with Japan and Italy in September. In it Japan agreed to recognize the leadership of Germany and Italy in the establishment of a new order in Europe as long as they recognized her new order in Asia.

Then came a series of setbacks: the loss of the bitter aerial Battle for Britain, the failure to mount Operation Sea Lion (the planned invasion of Britain), and two diplomatic reverses.

In early October Hitler met Mussolini again at the Brenner Pass and said his next goal was the root of the British Empire: Gibraltar. He was going to see Franco and get permission to transport German units across Spain to assault the Rock in an operation code-named Felix. Hitler complained that Franco was demanding too much grain and gasoline as their price for entry into the war against England. Franco, he said, was treating him "as if I were a little Jew who was haggling about the most precious possessions of mankind!" On October 23 he finally met the Caudillo at Hendaye, a French border town just below Biarritz.

For months Franco continued to stall Hitler, who finally, in disgust, abandoned the plan of capturing Gibraltar. Had Franco co-operated Hitler would have controlled the entire Mediterranean. Apart from the Caudillo's fear of aligning himself with a possible loser, there was a compelling motive for his decision to thwart Hitler: According to several sources—including the former British Ambassador to Spain, Sir Samuel Hoare—Franco was part Jewish.

On October 24, the day after his encounter with Franco, Hitler met with Marshal Henri Pétain, head of state of Vichy France, in Montoire. Once again he was frustrated: Pétain also, politely but firmly, refused to enter the war against England.

For Hitler it was a morose trip back to Germany. After his great victories in the West, the chief of a defeated power and the leader of a minor one were both refusing to be led into the crusade against England, and Hitler's own ally was stupidly endangering the Axis position in the Mediterranean to pursue personal glory on the battlefield. During the long train ride home the Führer railed at "deceiving" collaborators and ungrateful, unreliable friends.

120

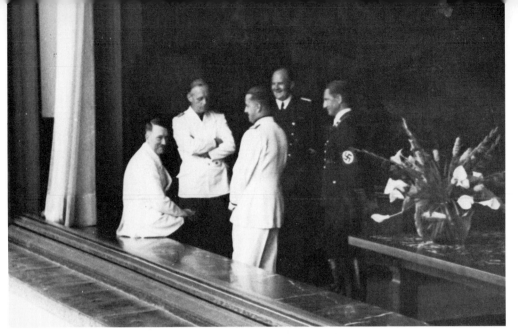

277. Hitler watching the Rolleiflex Girl as she records Ciano's visit. The Berghof's famed picture window could be lowered into the wall below.

278. Göring, Edda, and pet lion cub.

279. Rare candid picture of the family circle relaxing in the Berghof's "beer hall."

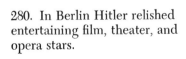

280. In Berlin Hitler relished entertaining film, theater, and opera stars.

281. That August Hitler and Stalin shocked the world by making an alliance.

282. WONDER HOW LONG THE HONEYMOON WILL LAST?

283. At the Berghof Hitler, flanked by Goebbels and Bormann, anxiously awaits word from Moscow. This picture was taken by Eva.

284. Hitler at the Reichstag on the morning of September 1, waiting to make his war speech.

285. "I will carry on this fight," he says, "no matter against whom, until the safety of the Reich and its rights are secured!"

286. Hitler watching his troops march into Poland.

287. After the battle of the Bzura, the Polish Army is completely annihilated. Caption to this photo in a Nazi propaganda book: "The Lord defeated them with horse, horseman and chariot!"

288. At Führer headquarters in Poland.

289. Hitler and General von Reichenau observe last phases of the battle for Warsaw through field glasses.

290. German troops goose-stepping through Warsaw after victory.

291. Polish Jews arrested after victory. Nazi caption: "Enemies of the German People."

292. Hitler's triumphal entry into Danzig on September 19. "Almighty God," he told a partisan crowd, "has now blessed our weapons."

293. Hitler speaking at the annual commemoration of the Beer Hall Putsch. "The fact that I left the Bürgerbräukeller earlier than usual," Hitler said afterward, "is a corroboration of Providence's intention to let me reach my goal." Wünsche, the ordnance office in charge of scheduling, stares at his chief from the front row.

294. The year ends as peacefully as it began. Hitler puts on a Christmas party for the children of Speer, Bormann, and others in the family circle.

295. Hitler takes time out to give the Ribbentrops a guided tour of the new Reich Chancellery.

296-97. He was planning another major conquest. In early 1940 in the old Reich Chancellery Hitler devised an invasion of the West. *Left*, Göring and Captain von Puttkamer, Hitler's naval adjutant, watching Hitler explain how to skirt the Maginot Line with tanks. Almost all his commanders opposed the unorthodox plan—which worked. *Right*, Keitl, Jodl, Schmundt (chief adjutant), and Puttkamer.

Miles scale: 0 — 200

Labels on map:

Narvik

SWEDEN

FINLAND

ATLANTIC
OCEAN

Namsos

Helsinki

Trondheim

Andalsnes

NORWAY

ESTONIA

Bergen

Oslo

Stockholm

Stavanger
Kristiansand

BALTIC
SEA

LATVIA

LITH.

Copenhagen

Danzig

E.
PRUSSIA

NORTH SEA

DENMARK

BOCK

Kiel

Warsaw

Wilhelmshaven

Hamburg

POLAND

Bremen

Berlin

RUNDSTEDT

GREAT
BRITAIN

Amsterdam
Antwerp
Brussels
Dunkirk

HOLLAND

GERMANY

Prague

London

BOCK

Dover

BELGIUM

SLOVAKIA

Abbeville

ARDENNES

RUNDSTEDT

ENGLISH CHANNEL

LUX.

Vienna

HUNGARY

Cherbourg

MAGINOT
LINE

LEEB

Munich

AUSTRIA

Paris

SEINE R.

Brest

SWITZERLAND

Venice

YUGOSLAVIA

Vichy

Milan

FRANCE

Lyon

ITALY

ADRIATIC
SEA

palacios

298. Victory in the west.

299. The fateful meeting at the Brenner Pass.

300. Nazi troops marching into Aalborg, Denmark.

301. The country falls with its navy never firing a shot and its land forces only managing to inflict twenty casualties on the invaders. But under occupation the Danes showed courage and saved their Jewish countrymen by transporting nearly all 6,500 of them to neutral Sweden. Here they cheer King Christian.

302. Hitler at his headquarters near the Holland-Belgian border, Rocky Nest, soon after launching his attack on the West.

303. The invasion is going well and Admiral Raeder brings up the possibility of invading England once France falls. Hitler is negative.

304. Following Hitler's plan, the German Blitz breaks through the French lines at Sedan and sweeps toward the English Channel—and Dunkirk.

305. German troops march into Dunkirk.

306. A French town destroyed.

307. A French column is caught on the bridge over l'Oise.

308. German troops parade down Avenue Foch in Paris, with the Arc de Triomphe in the background.

309–316. The jig that never was. Hitler's elation at news that France had surrendered was briefly filmed by Walter Frentz at Hitler's Belgium headquarters. The above frames (and there were no others, Frentz revealed to the author) were cleverly "looped" (repeated) by a Canadian film expert, making it appear that Hitler was executing a dance.

317. In the map room. Hitler hears more good news.

318. Hitler listens to a radio announcement of the Armistice at the Officers' Mess. The war with France is over.

321. Hitler meets Mussolini in Munich, June 19.

319. Sight-seeing in Paris.

320. Sentimental journey, June 1940. Hitler revisits his battlefields of 1914–18. "Never again trench warfare," he assures entourage.

322. The conqueror is welcomed home. July 1940. Note blackout hoods on the auto headlights.

323. From the balcony of the Reich Chancellery.

324. That September Hitler signs the Tripartite Pact with Japan and Italy. The Japanese bring gifts.

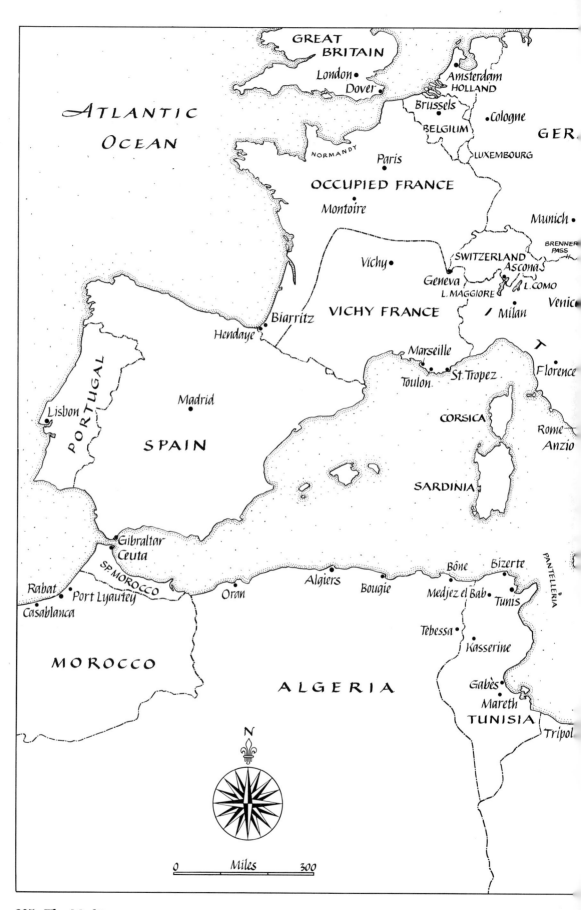

325. The Mediterranean.

326. The Battle
of Britain.

327. Göring, out of favor with the Führer after the loss of the Battle of Britain.

328. Franco's train arrived more than an hour late. "I'll have to use every trick I can," he told an adviser, "and this is one of them." At their meeting Franco avoided signing a treaty with Hitler and refused to accept Gibraltar as a present from foreign soldiers. That fortress, he insisted, must be taken by the Spaniards themselves. Hitler left Hendaye frustrated and enraged.

TEN

By Victory Undone

1940–1942

To the family circle, Hitler was a kindly father figure—a thoughtful employer who gave gold watches to those who ceased smoking, was sincerely interested in their welfare, and made at least one match between circle members. His relationship with Eva Braun had become more conjugal. Rather than separating them, the war brought them closer together, since he could now spend much more time at the Berghof. The routine there was strenuous, with luncheon served after 4 P.M. and dinner after 9, and most of Hitler's day filled with conferences. Later in the evening the guests would gather in the great hall where light refreshments would be served, and Hitler might play favorite records or lecture about the evils of tobacco, meat, or cosmetics. Sometimes the gathering did not break up until 4 in the morning.

After his failures with Franco, Pétain, and Mussolini, Hitler attempted to strengthen his ties with Stalin by drawing him into the Tripartite Pact. This scheme was the brain child of Ribbentrop, who saw an alliance of Germany, Italy, Japan, and the Soviet Union as the answer to European stability. Foreign Commissar Molotov promised to take the proposal back to Stalin but asked for so many concessions that Hitler was convinced that "sooner or later Stalin would abandon us and go over to the enemy." He decided irrevocably to do what he had talked about the last six months: invade Russia. He approved the plans in mid-December and gave the invasion a meaningful title: Operation Barbarossa (Red Beard) after Frederick I, the Holy Roman Emperor who had marched east in 1190 to take the Holy Land.

Late in March 1941 Hitler made a fatal decision. Concerned by the defeat of Italian troops in the Balkans, he decided to occupy that area. Only then, he said, would it be safe to launch Barbarossa. Twenty-nine German divisions were thrown into the Balkans campaign and within three weeks Yugoslavia was conquered and German tanks entered Athens. But of the huge German force only ten divisions saw action for

330. "Frettchen," Hansgeorg Schulze, Hitler's universally popular ordnance officer.

331. Eva snaps a smiling Sepp Dietrich, the commander of Leibstandarte SS Adolf Hitler—the bodyguard regiment. During the Röhm Putsch Dietrich had reluctantly presided over the executions of the top SA leaders.

329. Eva and Speer.

332. On the way to the teahouse. As usual Eva has her camera. The broadly smiling officer is Frettchen.

333. Hitler with Wolf.

334. A group walk in the spring of 1941.

335. Eva returned to Italy that summer. In Florence.

336. At Lake Garda in Italy.

337. On November 12, 1940, Foreign Commissar Molotov arrived in Berlin to talk of coalition.

338. Two faces of Adolf Hitler.

more than six days. A sledge hammer had been used to kill mosquitoes—and the opening of Operation Barbarossa was delayed for more than a month, a delay that would prove catastrophic.

On May 10 the security of Barbarossa seemed endangered when Rudolf Hess, Hitler's own deputy, flew to England in a quixotic effort to bring peace with England. It was a daring venture that ended in disaster for Hess. He was imprisoned by the English and reviled by the Nazis.

The day after learning about Hess, Hitler issued two repressive decrees. One declared that Russian civilians taking arms against the Wehrmacht in the coming invasion should be considered outlaws and shot without trial. The other empowered Himmler to carry out "special tasks which result from the struggle which has to be carried out between two opposing political systems." In plain words, Himmler was ordered to "cleanse" occupied Russian areas of Jews and other troublemakers by special SS murder squads, the *Einsatzgruppen*.

On the morning of June 22, 1941, Hitler finally launched Barbarossa. On that same day, 129 years before, Napoleon had crossed the Niemen River on his way to Moscow. Like Napoleon, Hitler advanced quickly on all fronts.

Millions of Russians were ready to greet Hitler as a liberator from the Stalinist terror, but Hitler, who from his youth considered Slavs as *Untermenscher*, listened to those advisers recommending harsh treatment of the conquered peoples—and turned them into bitter enemies. Following in the wake of the advancing German troops were four SS *Einsatzgruppen* of three thousand men each, whose mission was to prevent resistance by civilians. They were to round up and liquidate not only Bolshevik leaders but all Jews, as well as gypsies, "Asiatic inferiors," and "useless eaters," such as the deranged and incurable sick. The majority of *Einsatzgruppe* leaders were youngish intellectuals—a Protestant pastor, a physician, an opera singer, numerous lawyers—and it might be supposed

146

339–41. The Führer Train in the Balkans Campaign.

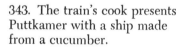

342. On April 20, 1941, the Führer's birthday, naval aide Puttkamer reports that he has been promoted to captain.

343. The train's cook presents Puttkamer with a ship made from a cucumber.

344. Bormann inspecting the train, which included a special car for the Führer's cow.

such men were unsuited for this work. On the contrary, they brought to the brutal task their considerable skills and training and became, despite qualms, efficient executioners. Most of the victims were Jews and the exterminations proceeded with cool calculation.

During that summer of 1941 covert preparations for the mass murder of Jews were also under way. Himmler summoned Rudolf Höss, commandant of the largest concentration camp in Poland, and gave him secret oral instructions. "He told me," Höss later testified, "something to the effect—I do not remember the exact words—that the Führer had given the order for the final solution of the Jewish question. We, the SS, must carry out that order. If it is not carried out now the Jews will later on destroy the German people." Himmler said he had chosen Höss's camp, since Auschwitz, strategically located near the border of Germany, afforded space for measures requiring isolation.

Until now the plans had been kept secret from Hitler's innermost circle—the secretaries, adjutants, servants, and personal staff. But that autumn the Führer began making open remarks during his evening table conversations. In mid-October he reminded his guests at the teahouse of his prophecy in the Reichstag that, if the Jews started a war, they would disappear from Europe. "That race of criminals has on its conscience the two million dead of the First World War, and now already hundreds and thousands more. Let nobody tell me that all the same we can't park them in the marshy parts of Russia. Who's worrying about our troops? It's not a bad idea, by the way, that public rumor attributes to us a plan to exterminate the Jews. Terror is a salutary thing."

345. Just before his flight, Hess and his son Wolf. The girl is Bormann's daughter. Hitler feared that Hess might have revealed the secret of Barbarossa to the British. He did not.

346. Two German soldiers amused at the hanging of Yugoslavian partisan.

The plan for Jewish extermination publicly rumored was soon to become fact. On May 1, 1942, Hitler left the eastern front to deliver a major speech to the Reichstag. He denounced Bolshevism as "the dictatorship of Jews" and labeled the Jew "a parasitic germ" who had to be dealt with ruthlessly. He demanded passage of a law granting him plenary powers. Every German was henceforth obliged to follow his personal orders—or suffer dire punishment. He was now officially above the law with the power of life and death. He had, in essence, appointed himself God's deputy and could do the Lord's work: wipe out the "Jewish vermin" and create a race of supermen.

By that spring six killing camps had been set up in Poland: Treblinka, Sobibor, Belzec, Lublin, Kulmhof, and Auschwitz. The first four gassed the Jews by engine-exhaust fumes, but Rudolf Höss, commandant of the huge complex near Auschwitz, thought this too "inefficient" and introduced to his camp a more lethal gas, hydrogen cyanide, marketed under the name of Zyklon B.

Against the advice of his generals Hitler ordered that the attack toward Moscow proceed on a wide rather than concentrated front. Panic

347. The swastika is raised over the Acropolis, with the Parthenon in background.

still swept the city and, at the Kremlin, Stalin had reputedly lost his nerve. Finally the Germans launched an all-out drive on the Soviet capital and came within sight of the city. But it was too late. Winter and the Red Army stopped the Nazis, and on December 6 Hitler admitted to General Alfred Jodl that "victory could no longer be achieved."

The following day the Japanese struck at Pearl Harbor. Four days later Hitler made another serious blunder: Instead of waiting for the United States to declare war on him, he convoked the Reichstag and said, "We will always strike first!"

The German retreat in the East threatened to degenerate into panicked flight by mid-December. Field Marshal von Brauchitsch, exhausted and depressed, wanted to continue the withdrawal but Hitler sent out a general order: "Stand fast, not one step back!" He fired Brauchitsch and took over personal command of the army.

He took time off from the Battle of Stalingrad to return to Munich and repeat once more his threat to exterminate the Jews of Europe. "People always laughed at me as a prophet," he told an enthusiastic audience at the Löwenbräukeller. "Of those who laughed then, *innumerable numbers* no longer laugh today, and those who laugh now will perhaps no longer laugh a short time from now. International Jewry will be recognized in its full demonic dangerousness; we National Socialists will see to that."

150

348. King Carol of Romania.

349. Admiral Horthy of Hungary.

350. Field Marshal Mannerheim of Finland.

351. Germany invades Russia: Panzer unit advances during the battle for Glosoff.

352. The German juggernaut advances along Russian highway.

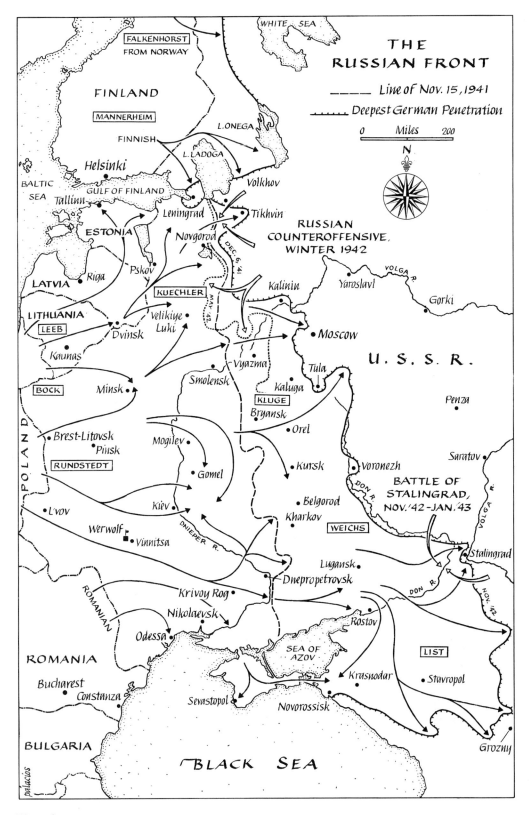

353. The Russian Front.

354. Hitler's troops win land and, at first, people: Ukrainians greet soldiers from the Leibstandarte SS Adolf Hitler with bread, salt, and smiles.

355. Within a month of the invasion's start Hitler had vetoed plans for a conciliatory approach to the people of the conquered territory.

356. Russian victims of the *Einsatzgruppen*.

357. Improvised insignia for an SS jeep on the Russian front.

358. Soviet poster linking Hitler and Napoleon: "That's the way it was . . . That's the way it will be!"

359. Ribbentrop with Hitler at his East Prussian headquarters—*Wolfsschanze*, Wolf's Lair.

360. The Officers' Mess. "Photo" Hoffmann gives General Schmundt, Hitler's chief adjutant, a sausage for his birthday.

362. Adjutants cooling off.

361. A lake near Wolf's Lair, the Moyensee.

363. Mussolini also came to Wolf's Lair that August and went on a flight over Russian lines. Moments after this photo was taken, he insisted on taking the controls from pilot Baur. Hitler consented to his regret. Il Duce maneuvered the plane with boyish élan.

364. That summer Hitler was grieved to learn of the death in battle of Hansgeorg "Frettchen" Schulze. He went up to the front to console Schulze's brother, Richard, who was also a member of the elite Leibstandarte Division, and offered him his brother's former position as aide. Here, Richard and Frettchen shortly before the latter's death.

365. Hitler inspects new helicopter.

366. Early winter, 1941, on the Russian front: Germans take prisoners.

367. The Russian front, December 1941. German propaganda photo: "The Bolshevik Winter Offensive —a mass enemy suicide." In fact, the Red Army was on the verge of crushing the Wehrmacht.

368. The SS Division, Das Reich, nears the Moscow suburbs.

369. December 7, 1941. Pearl Harbor.

370. Hitler's aides and adjutants hold a Christmas party at Wolf's Lair.

371. On February 15, 1942, after the military reverses in Russia of November—December 1941, Hitler exhorts recent SS officer graduates to stem the Red tide and save civilization. Behind: Schaub and Richard Schulze. The latter was so moved he wanted to go back to the front. The young lieutenants, he recalled, jumped onto their seats and cheered in a spontaneous demonstration.

372. A few days later Hitler lost his Minister of Armaments, the famed engineer Fritz Todt, in a mysterious plane crash at Wolf's Lair. Todt was replaced by architect Speer.

373. Hitler trains Blondie to leap over barriers.

374. Schulze helps arrange the Führer's birthday reception.

375. Reinhard Heydrich, chief of the dreaded SD, had just been appointed Acting Protector of Bohemia and Moravia. On May 27 he was fatally wounded in a grenade attack by two British-trained Czechs. In retaliation more than 1,300 innocent Czechs, including all the male inhabitants of Lidice (the town itself was razed), were executed with the two assassins.

376. In July 1942 Hitler moved east to Werewolf, the new headquarters in the Ukraine, so he could personally direct the attack on Stalingrad. Birthday celebration that August for Bormann's secretary, Fräulein Wahlmann. From left to right, Schaub, Hewel, Fräulein Wahlmann, Bormann, Engel, Fräulein Fugger (another Bormann secretary), and Heinrich Heim, instructed by Bormann to note down surreptitiously Hitler's table conversations.

377. A month later the inner circle celebrates Below's birthday. From left to right, Below (legs crossed), Christa Schröder (Hitler's secretary), Dr. Brandt, Hewel, Albert Bormann, Schaub.

378. By the end of 1942 disaster has struck in Egypt, where Rommel faces total defeat.

379. Another winter begins on the eastern front, and Hitler (with Bormann, left, at the Werewolf headquarters) faces an even greater disaster in Stalingrad where the entire Sixth Army was surrounded and doomed.

380. Germans surrendering on the eastern front.

ELEVEN

Into the Abyss

1943–1944

The year 1943 began with the last death struggle of General Friedrich Paulus' army surrounded at Stalingrad. On January 24 Hitler's spirits were momentarily lifted by the startling announcement that Roosevelt had called for the unconditional surrender of the Axis at the conclusion of an Allied conference in Casablanca. (For some time the Germans believed Casablanca was the code name for the White House and that the conference had taken place in Washington.) By making any political settlement of the world conflict quite impossible, the President had handed Hitler an invaluable piece of propaganda for resistance to the end.

Isolated groups of Germans inside Stalingrad were already surrendering in considerable numbers, but General Paulus himself stood firm and on January 30 sent Hitler greetings on the anniversary of his assumption to power. "The swastika still flutters over Stalingrad," he said, and in a personal message informed the Führer that the son of his half sister Angela, Leo Raubal, was wounded. Should he be evacuated by air? The reply was negative: As a soldier he must remain with his comrades. Thus the brother of Hitler's one true love, Geli Raubal, was consigned to almost certain death.

In April Hitler and Mussolini met at the baroque Klessheim Castle near Salzburg. Hitler was shocked by Il Duce's sunken cheeks and pallid face. In their talks, Mussolini was disspirited. The trouble with Il Duce, concluded Hitler, was age; he was sixty and in poor health.

On July 25 Il Duce resigned and was placed under arrest and held prisoner in a hotel near the top of Gran Sasso, the loftiest peak in the Apennines a hundred miles from Rome. At Wolfsschanze Hitler decided to act drastically, dramatically—and rescue his ally. An attack up the steep, rocky slope would not only cost many casualties but give the guards time to kill Mussolini. Parachuting into such terrain was almost as risky and so it was agree to use gliders.

To carry off this piece of derring-do, Hitler chose a fellow Austrian, SS Captain Otto Skorzeny, a Viennese who stood six-foot-four. He bore deep scars on his face from the fourteen duels he had fought as a student and carried himself with the air of a fourteenth-century condottiere. Not only a bold man of action but a canny one, he led his 107 men to a brilliant success on September 12. After overpowering the guards, Skorzeny escaped with Mussolini in a small Fieseler-Storch plane. In the meantime Skorzeny's men escaped by cable car, with the only casualties ten men injured in a glider crash.

In the meantime, Hitler was carrying out his plan to exterminate the Jews. Under Himmler's supervision the work of the six killing centers reached the peak of efficiency by the fall of 1943. The thought of refusing the Führer's order to murder apparently occurred to few, if any, of the executioners. "I could only say *Jawohl*," Höss, commandant of Auschwitz, later confessed. "It didn't occur to me at all that I would be held responsible. Don't you see, we SS men were not supposed to think about these things; it never even occurred to us. . . . We were all so trained to obey orders, without even thinking, that the thought of disobeying an order would simply never have occurred to anybody, and somebody else would have done it just as well if I hadn't."

Himmler's task was to train his men to become hard but not hardened; to murder and yet remain noble knights. They were to be gentlemen, in fact, no matter how atrocious their mission. And with this in mind, Himmler summoned his SS generals to Posen on October 4, 1943. His primary purpose was to enlarge the circle of those privy to the extermination of the Jews. The truth of the Final Solution was leaking out and Hitler had decided to involve the party and the military in his crime. By making them, in effect, coconspirators, he would force them to fight on to the end. If worse came to worst he would take millions of Jews with him.

This was the first in a series of information lectures by Himmler that were to include many civilian leaders and Wehrmacht officers. The first was the most important, since he must convince the SS that the execution of this distasteful deed was not at variance with the highest principles of their knightly order. "Among ourselves it should be mentioned once, quite openly, but we will never speak of it publicly. I mean the evacuation of the Jews, the extermination of the Jewish race." It had been, he said, the most onerous, distasteful assignment the SS ever had. "In the final analysis, however, we can say that we have fulfilled this most difficult duty for the love of our people. And our spirit, our soul, our character have not suffered injury from it."

The Jews were not the only victims of Hitler's New Order. Millions of others, particularly in occupied Russia, had been shot, gassed, and beaten to death. Hitler's policy of oppression included the ruthless starvation of Soviet prisoners of war. Alfred Rosenberg, Reich Minister of the East, himself bore witness to this inhumanity in a scorching letter to

381. The unconditional surrender announcement was a surprise to every-one but Churchill, who had heard Roosevelt use the phrase the pre-vious day at a private luncheon. Churchill had at first frowned, but then broke into a grin and said, "Perfect! And I can just see how Goebbels and the rest of them will squeal!"

Field Marshal Wilhelm Keitel. It charged that of the 3,600,000 Soviet prisoners of war only a few hundred thousand were in good health. The great majority had been starved or shot in a series of atrocities that, charged Rosenberg, ignored "potential understanding."

Countless other Soviet prisoners, along with non-Jewish inmates of concentration camps, were dying in a series of medical experiments: some after lying naked in snow or icy water; some during high-altitude tests; some as guinea pigs for mustard gas and poison bullets. Polish women at the Ravensbrück camp were inflicted with gas gangrene wounds; gypsies at Dachau and Buchenwald satisfied the curiosity of a group of doctors who wanted to know how long human beings could live on salt water.

The administration of occupied territories throughout Europe had

also resulted in manifold executions as reprisals for acts of sabotage and rebellion. These were legalized by Hitler on Pearl Harbor Day under the odd but apt title, "Night and Fog Decree." It ordered that all people endangering German security, except those to be executed immediately, were to "vanish" without leaving a trace. Their families were to be told nothing of their fate.

By the fall of 1943 Hitler's New Order in Western Europe, which purported to be an amalgamation of states for the common good, was revealed in its true nature: a plunder economy. Faced with millions reluctant to become mere vassals, Hitler turned from persuasion to sheer force. Acts of work stoppage and sabotage were answered by enforced labor and the execution of innocent hostages. In Holland and France the death toll was more than 20,000. Legalized pillage had become common with boxcars of loot (including food, clothing, and art treasures) converging on the homeland from Norway, Holland, Belgium, Luxembourg, France, and Denmark. This did not include enormous occupation assessments. France alone was paying seven billion marks a year for membership in the New Order.

While Hitler still envisaged grandiose plans of conquest encompassing five continents, the last six months of 1943 saw his armies in the East steadily driven back, as much as 250 miles in some places, and to the south his Italian ally's sudden collapse. In one year the Wehrmacht had suffered 1,686,000 casualties.

"If Providence should actually deny us victory," Hitler told a gathering of senior officers in January 1944, "then you, my generals and admirals, must gather around me with upraised swords to fight to the last drop of blood for the honor of Germany!" But usually Hitler preached a message of hope. Any day, he assured his companions at the Berghof, the situation would change entirely. The Anglo-Saxons would eventually re-

382. The Germans retreat on the Neval front.

383. Depressed by the debacle at Stalingrad, Hitler decides to leave dreary Wolf's Lair for the Berghof. He poses with his chauffeur, Kempka.

alize their best interest lay with his anti-Bolshevist crusade. At other times he boasted that the Western Allies would destroy themselves in front of the Atlantic Wall.

As the Allies raced across France, a group of German officers was planning to assassinate Hitler. On July 20 a bomb exploded under a conference table where he was mapping strategy. Hitler was saved when at the last moment an aide, trying to get a better look at the situation map, moved the brief case containing the bomb away from him.

Crushed to discover that the plot involved a large number of his officers, Hitler took to his bed. That August while still recuperating, Hitler received more bad news: Paris had fallen to the Allies and Bulgaria had withdrawn from the war. A few days later Romania was overrun by the Red Army and Finland was on the verge of surrender.

October brought a further defection. Miklós Horthy, the Hungarian admiral without a navy and the nominal ruler of a kingdom without a king, sent envoys to Moscow to beg for armistice. Hitler learned of this and sent his favorite commando, Skorzeny, to Hungary to bring its leaders back into line. In a imaginative operation code-named Mickey Mouse Skorzney kidnaped Horthy's son Miki, wrapped him in a carpet (Skorzeny got the idea from Shaw's play *Caesar and Cleopatra*), and delivered him to the airport. Then with a single parachute battalion he captured the citadel where Admiral Horthy lived and ruled. It took an hour.

Soon afterward Skorzeny was given a new assignment by Hitler: subvert enemy operations in a coming offensive in the Ardennes that, Hitler believed, would split the Americans and British both militarily and politically. Skorzeny was to train men to masquerade as GIs and wreak havoc behind the American lines.

The Battle of the Bulge came close to success, but by New Year's Eve, 1944, it had clearly failed.

384. Life on the Obersalzberg agrees with the Führer. He poses with his secretary, Johanna Wolf, on her birthday.

385. He celebrates his own on April 20. Photographer Hoffmann holds a present, and Herta Schneider, Eva's best friend, looks on.

386. Hitler's new secretary, Gertraud "Traudl" Humps. He encouraged her to marry his valet, Hans Junge.

387. Hitler had three relatives on the Russian front: Leo Raubal son of his half sister, Angela: Heinz Hitler, son of his half brother, Alois, Jr.; and Hans Hitler, whose father was the Führer's first cousin. Hans escaped to Germany; both Leo and Heinz were captured. According to Stalin's daughter, the Germans proposed exchanging her brother Yasha for one of the prisoners (it could have been either Leo or Heinz). But Stalin told her, "I won't do it. War is war." Reportedly young Stalin was shot by the Germans. Heinz Hitler died in captivity but Geli's brother returned home in 1955. Pictured: a Christmas card from Hitler to Heinz, his favorite nephew.

388. Hitler and Eva with dogs.

389. Eva wearing her grandmother's wedding dress.

390. Hitler and Eva with Uschi Schneider, Herta's daughter. The two Schneider girls were photographed so often with the couple that after war there were rumors that one of them was "Hitler's son."

391. Eva poses by a waterfall after swimming in the nude—a snapshot which would have infuriated the Führer.

392. Eva with Herta.

393. At Klessheim Castle, Mussolini shows silent doubt. During the conference Hitler compared himself favorably with Napoleon and at the luncheon table lectured his guests for an hour and forty minutes without interruption.

394. At the Berghof that July Hitler's three top adjutants—Engel, Schmundt, and Puttkamer—also look concerned. Hitler was about to set off for Italy for still another meeting with Il Duce. At this meeting near Feltre, their thirteenth, Mussolini fidgeted nervously as Hitler assailed the Italians for their defeatism.

395. Admiral Wagner, Göring, and Dönitz study map.

396. Escorted by Skorzeny, Mussolini was flown to Wolfsschanze, but upon landing the shattered dictator was reluctant to meet Hitler, and Skorzeny had to urge
him to leave the plane.

397. "You have performed a military feat which will become part of history,"
Hitler told Skorzeny. "You have given me back my friend Mussolini." This one
act of daring endeared Skorzeny to Hitler. The manner in which Mussolini had
been rescued not only raised German spirits but also captured the imagination
and admiration of much of the world, including their foes.

398. Ribbentrop escorts Mussolini at the Hitler headquarters.

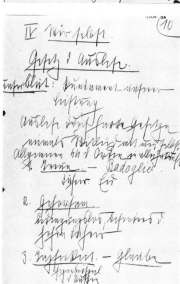

399. Pages from Himmler's outline for his October speech at Posen. Two days later he told a group of Gauleiters and Reichleiters, "The hard decision had to be taken—this people must disappear from the face of the earth." Himmler made some fifteen other speeches in the same vein to a wide range of audiences, including army and navy officers.

400. The Führer greets Himmler six days after the latter's first speech at Posen.

401. In the spring of that year, the Jews of the Warsaw Ghetto fought deportation to the death camps. The little Jewish army of 1,500 held out for four weeks until the last man was killed or wounded. SS General Stroop watches his troops burn the Ghetto.

402. Of the 56,065 who were rounded up, 7,000 were shot out of hand; 22,000 were sent to Treblinka and Lublin; the remainder to labor camps. The German losses were not heavy, but a severe blow had been dealt to Hitler's concept of "Jewish cowardice."

403. Nazi officials visit a concentration or killing camp. This photograph is notable for the resemblance of the man at the center to Hitler, and Himmler, right.

404. A few weeks before D-Day, Hitler and Mussolini say farewell—it would be their last—after conferring at Klessheim Castle. Moments later Mussolini confided to a diplomat that he had found Hitler's expectations for the war's outcome "devilishly optimistic!"

405. Field Marshal von Rundstedt inspects the defenses along the Atlantic Wall.

406. June 6, 1944: D-Day. Hitler was jubilant. "So, we're off!" he chuckled. "I am face to face with my real enemies!"

407. The bomb plot, July 20, 1944. Goebbels and Göring study wreckage of the conference table.

408. Major Otto Remer, promoted to major general by Hitler and given a division on the eastern front for his part in crushing the army bomb plot.

409. Hitler visits Puttkamer, who was injured in the blast.

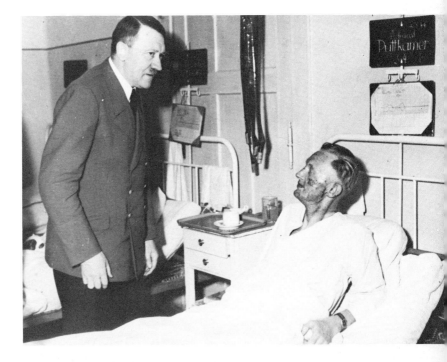

410. One of the few men Hitler now trusted was Dr. Erwin Giesing, who had treated him since the explosion. And Giesing, according to his diary, had once tried to kill Hitler, giving him a double dose of cocaine. Thinking he had killed the Führer, Giesing flew to Berlin only to learn that his attempt had failed and that no one was suspicious. The cocaine treatment was for a chronic headache Hitler suffered following the blast. Giesing persuaded Hitler to allow X rays of his skull to be taken. In 1977 Dr. C. W. Gehris, Jr., of Johns Hopkins Hospital commented that "the nasal septum in these X rays is fractured, consistent with sinusitis, which certainly sounds like the source of the headaches described, alleviated by cocainization."

411. Theo Morell, Hitler's chief doctor, is awarded a medal for his services to the Führer. Morell had been giving Hitler pills containing arsenic—through ignorance, not design. Dr. Giesing and other doctors in attendance exposed Morell's incompetence but Hitler would not listen. In 1945, however, he angrily dismissed Morell for suggesting that he take an injection of caffeine for his fatigue. "You will probably give me morphine!" Hitler shouted.

412. Joint funeral services in Budapest for the seven Hungarians and Germans who were killed during Operation Mickey Mouse. Skorzeny is at the far right.

413. Field Marshal Walter Model (right), Hitler's personal choice to command his last gamble, an offensive in the Ardennes, December 1944. Left, Bodenschatz; center, Luftwaffe General von Richtofen.

414. General Hasso von Manteuffel, (*above*) German pentathlon champion, whose tanks almost reached the Meuse River.

415. SS Colonel Peiper, whose tanks made the first deep break-through.

416. The New Year's party at Führer headquarters is a glum affair.

417. First the Americans are captured in great numbers.

418. Then the Germans.

TWELVE

The Last 100 Days of Adolf Hitler

1945

The personal leadership which had won Hitler such stunning victories early in the war now seemed to lead invariably to disaster. Himmler, with no military experience, was placed in command of an army group. Strategic withdrawals were forbidden, so that whole armies, including hundreds of thousands of men, were trapped behind enemy lines or annihilated. At almost every level National Socialist ineptitude or corruption was crippling government and industry. Meanwhile Hitler, who had taken on himself all responsibility for the conduct of the war and nation, was unwilling to see the situation in realistic terms, and veered between extremes of optimism and apocalyptic despair.

In choosing a successor Hitler had passed over Göring and Himmler, both of whom he considered disloyal for advocating surrender, to settle on Admiral Karl Dönitz. Realizing that the war was lost, the new German head of state set out to end hostilities as quickly as possible to prevent useless bloodshed. Himmler asked Dönitz to make him second man in the new government. "That is impossible," Dönitz said, "I have no job for you." The new Foreign Minister, Schwerin von Krosigk, suggested that Himmler take responsibility for the surrender of his SS troops, but instead he fled, poisoning himself after capture by the Allies two weeks later. Dönitz was unable to arrange a separate surrender on the western front, but in the forty-eight hours between the surrender's being signed and its taking effect thousands of German troops were able to make their way to western lines.

To the surprise of the world, Hitler's suicide a few days before the surrender brought an abrupt, absolute end to National Socialism. Without its only true leader, it burst like a bubble. There were no enclaves of fanatic followers bent on continuing Hitler's crusade; the feared Alpine Redoubt proved to be a chimera. What had appeared to be the most powerful and fearsome political force of the age had evaporated overnight. No other leader's death since Napoleon had so completely obliterated a regime.

419. American Secretary of State Stettinius proposes a toast at the end of the Yalta Conference in February, with Stalin, Roosevelt, Churchill, and Soviet Foreign Minister Molotov opposite. Conviction that a split in the alliance was imminent kept Nazi hopes alive.

420. The waiting room of the Führer bunker below the Reich Chancellery. Allied bombs had driven Hitler underground. Left edge, Dr. Morell; center, Hitler's former valet Krause and Admiral von Puttkamer.

421. Next to Bormann, the man Hitler saw most in these days was his favorite architect, Paul Giesler. They would spend many hours poring over illuminated wooden models of the new Linz, which would outrank Vienna as the jewel of Austria, or of a redesigned Munich (pictured). Hitler considered the Bavarian capital his true home: "Here I started my movement and here is my heart."

422. He visits the Oder front during the desperate days of mid-March. Hitler urged his commanders to contain the Russian drive on Berlin, promising that secret new wonder weapons would be ready momentarily.

423. On March 28 Chief of Staff Heinz Guderian, commander of the eastern front, angrily challenged Hitler's refusal to evacuate the army stranded in Kurland and was fired.

424. American soldiers climb the dragon's teeth tank obstacles of the Siegfried Line.

425. They captured books used in the public schools of Aachen during the Nazi regime.

426. East meets West. Cautious not to antagonize the Russians, Eisenhower held American forces back from Berlin and Prague, hampering Wehrmacht plans to surrender toward the West.

427–28. Many Germans are happy to surrender—at least to the Western allies.

429. Test pilot and ardent Nazi Hanna Reitsch flies with General Robert Ritter von Greim into besieged Berlin on April 26 and makes a forced landing on the broad avenue leading through the Brandenburg Gate. They urge Hitler to escape with them but he refuses.

430. On April 28 Hitler married Eva Braun. At left, their wedding certificate. Note errors: First, the date was smudged and then mistakenly altered to April 29; second, Eva started signing her maiden name before correcting herself so that a crossed out "B" precedes the "Hitler." After the ceremony Eva was radiant. She sent for the phonograph with its single record "Red Roses," and went out into the corridor to receive congratulations from the staff. Two days after saying their farewells to members of the inner circle, the couple secluded themselves in their private quarters. Eva took poison and Hitler shot himself in the right temple. Their bodies were carried to the garden of the Reich Chancellery and thoroughly cremated with gasoline.

431. The charred remains of Goebbels and his wife who after first poisoning their six youngest children had themselves shot by an SS orderly in the Chancellery garden. Himmler fled but took cyanide after capture.

432. Red flag is erected at the roof of the Reichstag.

433. Berlin is in ruins. The Reich Chancellery.

Overleaf: 434. Cologne in ruins.

SURRENDER

435. Three Hitler Youth, thrown into battle along with old men, are captured east of the Rhine.

436. German officer eating American C rations at Saarbrücken.

437. General von Trippelskirch and his aides.

438. A number of officers and civilians committed suicide rather than face defeat.

439. Field Marshal von Rundstedt.

440. Endless lines are surrendering.

441. VICTORY . . . Eisenhower a few minutes after the first signing of the German surrender at Rheims, May 7.

442. AND DEFEAT . . . Field Marshal Keitel at the second and final surrender ceremony in Berlin, May 8.

HORRORS OF THE FINAL SOLUTION REVEALED

443. German civilians are forced to see the prisoner dead at Buchenwald. On February 13, 1945, while dictating his last testament to Martin Bormann, Hitler said: "I have fought the Jews with an open visor. I gave them a final warning when the war broke out. I left them in no doubt that they would not be spared this time, should they once more thrust the world into war—that the vermin in Europe would be exterminated once and for all. . . . I have lanced the Jewish abscess, like the others. For this, the future will be eternally grateful to us." On April 2: "the world will be eternally grateful to National Socialism that I have extinguished the Jews in Germany and Central Europe."

444. German girl forced to watch exhumation of bodies at Namering.

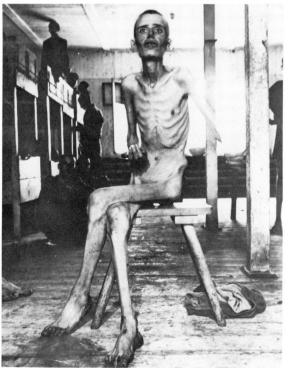

445. Slave laborers at Buchenwald.

446. Hungarian skeleton.

447. Crematoriums in German concentration camp at Weimar.

448. *"J'Accuse!"* A freed slave laborer points out a Nazi guard who brutally beat prisoners.

449. The Brandenburg Gate.

450. Allied soldiers at the emergency exit from Hitler's bunker, opening onto the blasted garden of the Reich Chancellery. Here the bodies of Hitler, Eva, and the Goebbelses were burned.

451. The picture window at the Berghof.

452. Hitler's tattered trousers from the July 20 bombing. They were kept in a U. S. Army vault for two years and then burned "to prevent their symbolic worship of what Hitler stood for."

453. Göring, Hess and Ribbentrop at the Nuremberg Trials. Of the twenty-eight major defendants only three (Schacht, Papen, and Fritzsche) were acquitted. Eight received long terms of imprisonment; the rest were sentenced to death. At 10:45 P.M., October 15, 1946, Göring cheated the hangman with a cyanide capsule. Two hours later the executions began.

454. When Hitler's SS adjutant, Otto Günsche (right), returned to West Germany after twelve years' imprisonment in the Soviet Union and East Germany, he was bewildered by the sight of young men with beards and long hair. "Dear friend," former Adjutant Schulze told him, "we have lost the war and all is now changed." Schulze took him to the Berghof. The remains of the building had been obliterated by the Americans. Everything looked different and it was difficult even to imagine where the long flight of steps leading up to the house had been. All trace of the most extraordinary figure in the history of the twentieth century had vanished—unlamented except by a blindly faithful few.

Acknowledgments

This picture book could not have been compiled without the co-operation of numerous people in Germany, Austria, England, and the United States. Archives and libraries contributed many photographs: The National Archives, Still Picture Branch (Joe Thomas, William Leary, Deborah Gilomer, Paul White); The Library of Congress; The Imperial War Museum (Rose Coombs, Mike Willis); The Bayerisches Hauptstaatarchiv, Munich; the Bibliothek für Zeitgeschichte, Stuttgart (Dr. Jurgen Rohwer, Werner Haupt); and the Bundesarchiv, Koblenz.

Numerous agencies, organizations, and individuals also contributed to this book: The Department of the Army, Washington, D.C.; Central Military History Office, Department of the Army (Charles MacDonald, Marian Mc'Naughton); Munin-Verlag, Osnabruck, publishers of *Wenn all Bruder Schweigen*; Max Wünsche; SS Major Otto Günsche, General Hasso von Manteuffel; SS Colonel Otto Skorzeny; Colonel Hans Ulrich Rudel; Colonel Edward Schaefer; Glen Sweeting; Monika and Richard Schulze-Kossens; Ben E. Swearingen; Harry Schulze-Wilde; Dr. Eleonore (Kandl) Weber; Edward Whalen; Dr. Walter Schultze; Nerin Gun; Dave Staton; Rogan Showalter; Jakob Tiefenthaler; Egon Hanfstaengl; Leni Riefenstahl; Rev. Bernard Strasser; Walter Frentz; General Walter Warlimont; and General Otto Remer.

Special thanks are due to Hildegard Fath for the Hess Family collection; Albert Speer for the Hitler sketches; Furmin Michel for his Göring and Schaub collection; Hans Hitler for the family pictures and documents; Wolfgang Glaser for his pictures of Hitlerland Today; Dr. Rudolph Binion for information regarding Dr. Bloch's cancer treatment of Frau Hitler; Erich Kempka for his candid photos of Hitler; Admiral Karl Jesko von Puttkamer for his Führer Headquarters collection; and Frau Herta Schneider for her Eva Braun albums. I would also like to thank my chief research assistant in Germany, Karola Gillich; Edward Weiss; and my Doubleday editors: Carolyn Blakemore, Ken McCormick, and

John Stillman. Finally, my greatest benefactor has been the United States Government which gave me the pick of hundreds of thousands of photographs from 279 captured Nazi albums. At the Library of Congress there are the 47 personal albums of Hermann Göring which go back to his career as a fighter pilot in World War I. At the National Archives are three magnificent collections: the 33 personal albums of Eva Braun, Hitler's mistress of some thirteen years and wife of less than two days; the 68 personal albums of Joachim von Ribbentrop, Hitler's Foreign Minister; and the 131 albums of Heinrich Hoffmann, Hitler's personal photographer from 1923 until the end of the Third Reich. Thousands of these photographs have never been published outside of Hitler's Germany. Hundreds have never been published anywhere.

CREDITS

Photographs identified solely by reference number are from the National Archives.

1. No credit.
2. Dr. Eleonore (Kandl) Weber.
3. Library of Congress.
4. Hans Hitler.
5. Library of Congress.
6. Hans Hitler.
7. Hoffmann.
8. Bundesarchiv.
9. No credit.
10. Palacios, Doubleday.
11. No credit.
12. Schulze-Wilde.
13. Schulze-Wilde.
14. Schulze-Wilde.
15. Toland.
16. Schulze-Wilde.
17. 242-HB-590.
18. Library of Congress.
19. Schulze-Wilde.
20. U. S. Army.
21. Toland.
22. No credit.
23. Bundesarchiv.
24. Toland.
25. Toland.
26. U. S. Army.
27. U. S. Army 32239.
28. U. S. Army 1076.
29. U. S. Army 1081.
30. Bundesarchiv ABC-3373.
31. Bundesarchiv.
32. No credit.
33. U. S. Army.
34. Bernhard Strasser.
35. Toland.
36. Bibliothek für Zeitgeschichte.
37. 242-HB-9027.
38. Festschrift.
39. Bundesarchiv.
40. Bundesarchiv.
41. No credit.
42. 242-HMA-632.
43. 242-HMA-1008.
44. 242-HMA-003.
45. Library of Congress.
46. 242-HB-18499.
47. 242-HB-2274.
48. 242-HMA-2400.
49. Hauptstaadt Archiv.
50. U. S. Army.
51. Imperial War Museum.
52. National Archives.
53. Imperial War Museum.
54. National Archives.
55. 242-HMA-2733.
56. 242-HMA-2766.
57. 242-HMA-2438A.
58. 242-HMA-2374.
59. National Archives.
60. Library of Congress.
61. No credit.
62. Hans Hitler.
63. National Archives.
64. Schulze-Wilde.
65. Rogan Showalter.
66. Imperial War Museum.
67. Library of Congress.
68. Hanfstaengl.
69. No credit.
70. U. S. Army.
71. U. S. Army.
72. 242-HAR-2-30B.

73. 242-HMC-3803.
74. Firmin Michel Collection.
75. Library of Congress.
76. 242-HAP-1928-17C.
77. 242-HAP-1928-11A.
78. 242-HAP-1928-11C.
79. 242-HF-304.
80. G. Sweeting.
81. 242-HB-2887.
82. National Archives.
83. 242-HF-309.
84. 242-HB-4066B.
85. Schulze-Wilde.
86. 306-NT-865G-7.
87. Toland.
88. Hans Hitler.
89. Hans Hitler.
90. Dave Staton.
91. Library of Congress
92. 242-EB-24-4.
93. 242-EB-24-5.
94. 242-EB-31-26A.
95. 242-EB-24-6B.
96. 242-EB-11-40A.
97. 242-EB-31-45B.
98. 242-EB-33-27A.
99. 242-EB-5-45.
100. 242-EB-24-13A.
101. 242-EB-1-45B.
102. 242-EB-1-43E.
103. Imperial War Museum.
104. 306-NT-112-458.
105. Library of Congress.
106. National Archives.
107. 242-HB-1121.
108. 242-HB-5167.
109. 242-HB-49.
110. Stadtarchiv, Munich.
111. No credit.
112. U. S. Army.
113. U. S. Army.
114. Hans Hitler.
115. Bundesarchiv.
116. 242-EB-28-6C.
117. U. S. Army.
118. 306-NT-865-6.
119. 242-HB-3835.
120. 242-HB-2747.
121. 306-NT-176413C.
122. 306-NT-864-20.
123. 242-HB-2748.
124. 306-NT-865-10.
125. 306-NT-176664.
126. 242-HB-1171.

127. 306-NT-178018C.
128. 242-HB-1877a.
129. 242-HB-998.
130. 242-HB-1019.
131. 242-HB-67.
132. 242-EB-23-32A.
133. 242-HB-1339.
134. 306-NT-870-8.
135. No credit.
136. Toland.
137. Hanfstaengl.
138. Hanfstaengl.
139. 306-NT-865-R-1.
140. Stadtarchiv, Munich.
141. Ben Swearingen.
142. 242-HB-7069.
143. 242-HB-2506.
144. 306-NT-340-WW-3.
145. 306-NT-340-WW-1.
146. 242-HB-4925.
147. 242-5564A.
148. 242-HB-3849.
149. 242-HB-3851.
150. 306-NT-395-52.
151. 242-HB-6694.
152. 305-NT-969-30.
153. 242-HB-6862-a1.
154. 242-HB-6677.
155. 242-HB-7385.
156. 242-HB-7421.
157. 242-HB-7494.
158. 242-EB-29-8A.
159. 242-EB-1-33D.
160. G. Sweeting.
161. 242-HB-7313A8.
162. 242-HB-7675.
163. 242-HB-7677.
164. 242-HB-8199a509.
165. 242-HB-8199a152.
166. 242-HB-8199a261.
167. Speer Archiv.
168. 242-HB-8199a43.
169. 306-NT-870-11.
170. 242-HB-7727, 242-HB-7736.
171. 242-JRA-2-5.
172. 242-HB-6978a18.
173. 242-HB-6978a13.
174. 242-HB-19418.
175. 306-NT-870-9.
176. Fath.
177. Fath.
178. Fath.
179. Fath.
180. Fath.

181. Hanfstaengl.
182. 242-HB-2.
183. 242-HB-129.
184. 242-HB-21857.
185. Firmin Michel Collection.
186. Library of Congress.
187. Library of Congress.
188. 242-HB-31674-43.
189. Firmin Michel Collection.
190. Library of Congress.
191. Library of Congress.
192. 242-EB-9-25.
193. 242-EB-1-171B.
194. 242-EB-1-36A.
195. 242-EB-1-37D.
196. 242-EB-2-11A.
197. Fr. Schneider.
198. 242-EB-1-41D.
199. Kempka.
200. Speer Archiv.
201. No credit.
202. 242-EB-12-12A.
203. 242-EB-12-2.
204. E. Baumann.
205. 242-EB-11-11A.
206. Frentz.
207. 242-EB-6-13C.
208. 242-EB-22-33B.
209. 242-EB-11-12A.
210. 242-EB-11-12B.
211. 242-EB-11-19A.
212. 242-EB-11-13B.
213. 242-EB-11-40B.
214. U. S. Army.
215. 242-JRA-11-29.
216. 242-HB-21919-3.
217. 242-HB-3528.
218. 242-HB-21299-1.
219. 242-HB-22280-1.
220. 208-AA-2030-3.
221. 242-HB-4825.
222. 242-HB-2769.
223. 208-N-39828.
224. National Archives.
225. 242-HB-2193.
226. 208-AA-203G-8.
227. Degrelle.
228. 306-NT-865-2.
229. Kempka.
230. Kempka.
231. Kempka.
232. U. S. Army.
233. 306-NT-865K-12.
234. 80-G-410205.

235. Library of Congress.
236. 306-NT-865N-1.
237. Breker.
238. Breker.
239. Speer Archiv.
240. Speer Archiv.
241. Speer Archiv.
242. Speer Archiv.
243. Speer Archiv.
244. Speer Archiv.
245. Speer Archiv.
246. 242-EB-6-7.
247. 242-EB-3-2.
248. 242-HB-6250-1.
249. 242-HB-3877.
250. 306-NT-969-18.
251. 306-NT-969-3.
252. 306-NT-969-33.
253. 242-JRB-1-75.
254. 242-EB-4-41B.
255. 242-EB-5-2D.
256. 242-EB-2-41E.
257. 242-EB-4-43B.
258. 242-EB-28-12D.
259. Wünsche.
260. Wünsche.
261. 242-EB-28-26B.
262. U. S. Army 585 662.
263. Imperial War Museum.
264. 306-NT-948E.
265. 306-NT-865c-3.
266. Library of Congress.
267. 242-GAP-303K-1.
268. 242-JRB-7-8.
269. 242-JRB-8-5.
270. 242-JRB-28-41F.
271. 242-EB-6-4.
272. 306-NT-128917.
273. 306-NT-129057C.
274. 306-NT-182760.
275. 242-JRB-20-29.
276. 242-EB-6-11B.
277. 242-EB-6-28.
278. Library of Congress.
279. Firmin Michel Collection.
280. Firmin Michel Collection.
281. 242-JRB-26-38.
282. Library of Congress.
283. 242-EB-6-41C.
284. 242-JRB-27-51.
285. 306-NT-1222E.
286. Imperial War Museum.
287. G. Sweeting.
288. 242-JRB-28-9.

289. 131-NO-2-100.
290. G. Sweeting.
291. G. Sweeting.
292. 306-NT-132A-A-7.
293. Bibliothek für Zeitgeschichte.
294. 242-EB-8-5c.
295. 242-JRB-41-23.
296. Puttkamer.
297. Puttkamer.
298. Palacios, Doubleday.
299. 242-JRB-41-27.
300. 242-GAP-17A-6.
301. 242-GAP-17CC-2.
302. Puttkamer.
303. Puttkamer.
304. 242-GAP-61B-2.
305. G. Sweeting.
306. G. Sweeting.
307. G. Sweeting.
308. G. Sweeting.
309. Transit Film Munich.
310. Transit Film, Munich.
311. Transit Film, Munich.
312. Transit Film, Munich.
313. Transit Film, Munich.
314. Transit Film, Munich.
315. Transit Film, Munich.
316. Transit Film, Munich.
317. Bibliothek für Zeitgeschichte.
318. Puttkamer.
319. National Archives.
320. Puttkamer.
321. 242-JRB-37-13.
322. 242-EB-7-47.
323. U. S. Army.
324. 242-HB-22250-1.
325. Palacios, Doubleday.
326. 306-NT-2743V.
327. Firmin Michel.
328. 242-JRB-47-29.
329. 242-EB-27-166.
330. 242-EB-13-2C.
331. 242-EB-11-5C.
332. 242-EB-27-15E.
333. 242-EB-13-36B.
334. 242-EB-13-1.
335. 242-EB-3-40B.
336. 242-EB-15-13C.
337. Library of Congress.
338. Puttkamer.
339. 242-HB-46581-7.
340. 242-HB-46581-17.
341. 242-HB-46581-27.
342. Puttkamer.

343. Puttkamer.
344. Firmin Michel Collection.
345. Fath.
346. Library of Congress.
347. G. Sweeting.
348. 242-JRB-9-39.
349. 242-HB-61900-224.
350. 242-HB-48400-183.
351. 200(S)-GT-173.
352. 242-GAV-96.
353. Palacios, Doubleday.
354. 242-GAV-106B.
355. 242-GAV-43B.
356. 242-SS-11-21-18.
357. 242-SS-11-32-39.
358. 200(S)-G-104.
359. U. S. Army.
360. Puttkamer.
361. Puttkamer.
362. Puttkamer.
363. Puttkamer.
364. Schulze; also in National
    Archives, 242-EB-13-7.
365. 242-HB-48400-411.
366. 242-SS-10-101-6.
367. G. Sweeting.
368. Munin Verlag.
369. U. S. Army.
370. Puttkamer.
371. Schulze.
372. Puttkamer.
373. Puttkamer.
374. 242-EB-14-2A.
375. 242-HBA-5948.
376. Puttkamer.
377. Puttkamer.
378. U. S. Army.
379. 242-HB-48400-5300.
380. 306-NT-1334-12.
381. U. S. Army.
382. 306-NT-1334-14.
383. 242-HB-48400-89.
384. 242-EB-11-24.
385. 242-EB-13-25.
386. Gertraud Junge.
387. Hans Hitler.
388. 242-EB-14-7A.
389. 242-EB-25-53.
390. 242-EB-13-40A.
391. No credit.
392. 242-EB-11-29.
393. 242-HB-48400-641.
394. Puttkamer.
395. Puttkamer.

396. Tiefenthaler.
397. 242-HB-48400-932.
398. 242-HB-48400-926.
399. National Archives.
400. U. S. Army.
401. 238-NT-289.
402. 238-NT-298.
403. National Archives.
404. U. S. Army.
405. U. S. Army.
406. U. S. Army.
407. Puttkamer.
408. Remer.
409. Puttkamer.
410. Schulze.
411. 242-HB-61900-172.
412. Skorzeny.
413. U. S. Army.
414. Manteuffel.
415. Peiper.
416. Puttkamer.
417. U. S. Army.
418. U. S. Army.
419. U. S. Army.
420. Puttkamer.
421. Frentz.
422. Bibliothek für Zeitgeschichte.
423. 200(S)-GT-64.
424. U. S. Army.
425. U. S. Army.

426. U. S. Army.
427. U. S. Army.
428. U. S. Army.
429. 242-HB-222494-18.
430. Dwight D. Eisenhower Library.
431. Sovfoto.
432. Sovfoto.
433. Firmin Michel Collection.
434. 239-RC-18-1.
435. U. S. Army 204587.
436. 208-YE-145.
437. U. S. Army 205637.
438. 208-YE-148.
439. U. S. Army 207633.
440. U. S. Army 207207.
441. Culver Pictures.
442. U. S. Army 206291.
443. U. S. Army 203472.
444. 208-YE-1B-12.
445. Signal Corps, U. S. Army
446. 208-AA-12764.
447. Signal Corps, U. S. Army
448. U. S. Army 203466.
449. U. S. Army 210303.
450. 208-PU-932-23.
451. 208-PU-932-22.
452. U. S. Army 304-534.
453. 306-NT-1378A-6.
454. Monika Schulze-Kossens.

COLOR SECTION

I. U. S. Army.
II. U. S. Army.
III. U. S. Army.
IV. Toland.
V. Toland.
VI. U. S. Army.
VII. Toland.
VIII. U. S. Army.
IX. Toland.
X. Toland.
XI. U. S. Army.